# From Colored Town to Pebble Beach

## The Story of the Singing Sheriff

by Pat DuVal

Carmel, California

June 2014

This book is the life story of Pat DuVal. It is based on his own memory, and conversations with people from his past and from today. To the best of his knowledge, the information in this book is true, within the margins of human memory.

# From Colored Town to Pebble Beach

## The Story of the Singing Sheriff

### All Rights Reserved

ISBN-13: 978-1499757507

ISBN-10: 1499757506

Printed in the United States of America

# *Table of Contents*

# *Publisher's Note*

When Pat DuVal gave me his manuscript, it was with trepidation. He had serious doubts about whether his story was something people would want to read. As you will see, his life's story is both interesting in its own right and important in illuminating the historic changes that have taken place for blacks in America.

We chose to limit the editing to preserve his style of recounting, which was more like a pilot's log than a narrative. But what he relates of what happened in his life is compelling, starting as a young child in a segregated community on the Atlantic Coast of Florida, leading through his teen and young adult years, into his time in the military, and then moving into his adulthood when he became a sheriff's deputy in Monterey County where he patrolled such very rich, white communities as Pebble Beach and Carmel.

Thanks go to Denise Swenson for her work on the manuscript, and her suggestions that helped to make the book a more comprehensive account of a significant life. Thanks as well to Eye Goddess Jules Hart for her editorial assistance.

Tony Seton
Carmel, California

# *Acknowledgments*

It was some time in the early nineties when I was singing at Neil DeVaughn's, a landmark restaurant on Cannery Row, when who should walk in but Maya Angelou. She was touring, and she had heard about me. She was introduced to me and she said, "I came to hear the singing sheriff." And the place got quiet as people looked up and recognized her.

We sang from "Porgy and Bess" with Steve Tosh playing the piano. We had a great time. She asked me how I got here and I told her my story. She said, "You need to take notes and write a book."

So thank you, Maya Angelou, and to my other friends who encouraged me in this effort, especially Hugo Gerstl, Shelby Steele, Armand Kunde, and Peter Baldwin.

# *Author's Note*

I'm actually surprised that this book is getting published. Some friends who'd heard I'd "written a book" encouraged me to do something with it. Several of them suggested that I get in touch with Tony Seton because he had published books of people that I knew plus many of his own.

I gave him my manuscript which he told me he'd take a look at. When he called me just two days later, I was sure he was going to tell me that it wasn't worth the bother. But instead, he told me that he had read the whole book, and though it needed some work, he thought it should be edited and published.

The content of the book is like I wrote it. Tony said it should be in my words and how I had said things. I know he spent a long time on cleaning it up though, and to make it more readable. He kept true to that, and I am most grateful.

For more of my story and the latest about my singing career, please visit my website, TheSingingSheriff.com.

Pat Duval
June 2014

# *Preface*

Most people don't realize the vast changes in the lives of blacks in America that have taken place in just the past fifty years, but I actually lived them. I was born into the old way and thankfully lived in the new. Let me give you a picture of what it was like before blacks were legally entitled to their civil rights.

Black people, who lived in the Deep South during the Jim Crow era – from the end of the Civil War to the passage of the Civil Rights Act of 1965 – were constant victims of racism and prejudice. Conditions were so bad that many blacks left their homes and migrated to the North seeking jobs and hoping for a better life. Most of this migration took place at the turn of the century. Life was better in the North, but racism existed there, too, of course, but it was less prevalent and far less violent.

Some who migrated to the cities like Chicago, New York, Detroit, and other cities, managed to get better jobs. Some worked on the assembly lines at Ford, General Motors and American Motors. It was far better than working in the cotton fields, plowing with a mule, and living in old single-walled shanties, provided by the white boss. Blacks were easily taken advantage of, especially in the South, because most were illiterate.

Many were sharecroppers who were supposed to share the profits at the end of the season or year, but that almost never happened. The white owner would report that there had been no profits. As a result, the workers continued to live on the plantations or farms working for almost nothing because they could not afford to leave. Some of the blacks seemed to have been satisfied with that type of life, but it was mostly because they didn't know better or didn't have a choice.

Usually, the wife of the sharecropper would work in the white boss's home doing the cooking, cleaning, and caring for their children. Afterwards, she had to come home to do the same tasks for her own family.

Black folk – they were referred to as "colored" in those days; when people were being polite – did not have the luxury of buying food, such as steaks. Instead, they subsisted on animal parts that the white folks didn't want, like organ meat from hogs. But let me add that many creative cooks managed to make tasty dishes of what they had.

There were no black doctors and most white doctors would not treat blacks. If the white doctors did see black patients, it was through a waiting room in the rear of their facility, and it was after he was done with the whites. For health care, blacks relied mostly on old remedies that had been handed down for generations and were administered to the children by their parents. So if a black had ringworm, an iron bar would be heated and placed on the infected area. Then the patient would swallow a few drops of kerosene or turpentine on a teaspoon full of sugar. For a chest cold or fever, a mustard plaster would be applied to the chest; then he patient would be wrapped in a quilt or a thick blanket. A bee sting was treated by applying snuff someone had chewed right onto the site of the sting. These remedies usually worked, and quickly, often with the person cured by the next day.

Both public and Catholic schools were segregated, and although they were supposedly equal, the white students always had better facilities, books, desks, and food service.

Public recreational facilities, such as parks and public libraries, could not be used by blacks, even though they were taxpayers.

God knows how many blacks were cheated by mortgage lenders, a practice that goes on to this day. The biggest problem then was the inability of blacks to read.

The jails were also segregated. In Florida, whites were housed on one side of the jail, and blacks and Seminole Indians on the other.

The segregation in the Deep South was obvious in the fact that there were "Colored Towns." Blacks could not buy property outside of the them. Black policemen had the authority to arrest blacks but not whites. If a white committed a crime in one of the Colored Towns, then a white policeman would come out to do the investigation. A white policeman could patrol in Colored Town at any time but you would never see a black policeman in a white community.

Black and white policemen did not patrol together. Police offices were segregated. The courthouse had a separate area where blacks could sit. There was no mingling with whites.

Public transportation, such as buses, were segregated. Blacks had to sit in the back, behind a white line on the floor. Even if the seats for the whites were empty, blacks would still have to stand in the back of the bus. White bus drivers were known to be rude to blacks, and a number of them in my community had a reputation of assaulting elderly blacks.

Blacks becoming part of the armed forces during the Second World War was a major step in desegregation, but after the war, blacks coming home found that little had changed for veterans and their families in the Deep South. Everything was still segregated. Living conditions were still the same, if not worse. Yes, things were a little better for them up North but there was still oppression in places. For instance, the massive Levittown housing development on Long Island was for whites only.

In the North, veteran blacks usually found better jobs, especially in the burgeoning automotive industry, but the veteran who returned to the South had nothing to look forward to. Cotton, tomato, and bean fields, along with citrus groves, had no modern machinery to do harvesting. Most of the farm labor was done by hand. In the citrus groves, the small trees were fertilized by hand. Each worker would have a large hemp bag strapped to his body, filled with fertilizer. He then would be assigned a row of trees to fertilize, where he had to scatter two to three handfuls at the roots of each tree. The black laborer was paid less than a dollar an hour for this work.

During the Jim Crow Era, some black businessmen thrived, but only in Colored Town. There were grocers, dry cleaners, insurance agents, and clothiers among others. Of course, black businessmen could only operate within the boundaries of Colored Town, though a white businessman could come into Colored Town and establish any kind of business he desired, and most of the major businesses in the center of Colored Town were owned by whites.

Most white clothiers would not allow a black to try on clothes. They could make a purchase, providing they did not have to put the garments on. Returning merchandise was out of the question.

Restaurants did not cater to blacks. Most kitchen employees were black, but they were never the busboys or waiters. White folks didn't want blacks around when they were eating.

Blacks shopping or working downtown, when they

wanted to eat, they would have to bring their lunch with them. Some restaurants had an outside alley way that led to the kitchen. There might be a counter at the cook's window and maybe some stools. There was usually a large exhaust fan overhead. The "diners" would pay the cook for a meal.

Most of these outside alleys were amidst dirty old sheds and discarded junk and garbage. Whoever ate at these counters had to shoo away flies, mosquitos, and cockroaches. During the summers, it was hot and humid, and the during the winters, dining *al fresco* at these black "restaurants" was particularly unpleasant in the very cold.

There were separate water fountains with "Whites Only" or "Colored" signs attached to each. If the black fountain was out of order, he better not use the white side. If he was caught, he could be fined, or worse. The same with public restrooms. Well into the Sixties those signs were up throughout the South, despite the new laws, and local justice was still meted out, and with anger.

For blacks in the Deep South, it was awful in every respect. Always, we wondered whether life would get any better. Even when I left Fort Pierce in 1964, the library, public schools, and everything else were still segregated.

# *I Never Thought...*

I was born in Fort Pierce, Florida, November 15, 1942. Segregation was a way of life for me. Growing up how could I help but think that the white man ruled the world... and he always would. That's just the way it was.

I never thought that I would ever see schools in the Deep South integrated. Nowadays, most schools and colleges are. I attended a diverse junior college in Monterey, California. Back then, they used "diverse" instead of "integrated."

I never thought that I would see black and white policemen patrolling together. Or see a black policeman listening to a white person's problems, or arresting a white. I was the first black sheriff's deputy in Monterey County, California.

I never thought that I would ever be served at a lunch counter owned by a white person. Nor did I ever think that I would eat in an upscale restaurant.

I never thought that I would live in an affluent white community.

I never thought that I would ever become a member of Carmel Valley Rotary and a board member of other organizations. I did a lot of singing at fundraisers for them.

I never thought that I would be able to worship in the same church as white people. But I have not only worshipped, I have sung in the many of churches that were once white..

I never thought that I would sing in a large chorus

accompanied by a symphony orchestra. But I not only performed as a choral member, I also became an accomplished soloist.

I never thought that I would perform with celebrities that I used to listen to on the radio – it was just part of my "silly dream" – when I was a youngster, but in fact I've performed with some top-name stars.

I never thought that I would ever learn to play golf. Blacks were not allowed to play on our local course when I was growing up. Later on, I did learn to play in Pebble Beach, on some of the world's most exclusive courses.

I never thought I would ever see black athletes playing professional sports. As a teenager, I saw Jim Brown and Big Daddy Lipscomb during the fifties. In person, I saw black members of the Brooklyn Dodgers when they were down for a spring training camp in nearby Vero Beach, Florida.

I never thought I'd see a black person anchoring a television news show, but eventually I did. It was Belva Davis on a San Francisco station.

It's no wonder they tell y*ou to never say never.

# *My Early Years*

Fort Pierce, Florida is a town on the Intercoastal Waterway located fifty miles north of the very rich, white Palm Beach, and fifty miles south of Cape Canaveral. My father was Patrick and my mother was Anne.

A few weeks after I was born, my dad was drafted into the army along with his friend, David Monroe. While my dad was in the Army, we lived with Mrs. Plummer, a friend of my maternal grandmother, Annabelle. I can recall being afraid of her, as she was meaner than a peach orchard bull.

My mom was a petite woman. She was just over five feet tall and weighed only 98 pounds. She had long curly hair.

One day when I was about two months old, as she told me later, she was pushing me down Eighth Street in a large baby carriage. She was met by a little woman named Mrs. Driver. She was a very nice woman who then was probably in her eighties. She said to my mother, "Anne Clara, let me see your baby." As she was touching my face with her withered fingers, she said, "This boy is going to be a famous singer someday; I can tell by the shape of his little round mouth. You just wait and see." Mom replied jokingly, "If he should become rich and famous, he can take care of me and his dad."

My Mom was a domestic worker for a white family. She only did their laundry and ironed their clothes. We did not have a car so the white woman would come to get us; my mother took me with her. We had to ride in the back seat of her car as we were not allowed to sit in the front seat with her.

Whenever my mom had to work and could not take me with her, she would leave me with a family friend, Josephine Davis. Everyone called her Josephine Blue, because her husband was so black, he was blue. His nickname was "Blue." They never had children. She would buy comic books for me so she could teach me to read. She was large in stature, a heavy smoker, and had a loud, heavy voice. She was a very good cook and worked at a local truck stop. I would cry whenever I had to leave her.

We later moved in with my grandmother. She had eight fingers; four on each hand. She had fallen against the top of a glass table and severed two fingers. Grandmother Annabelle lived across the street from the Baptist church on Eighth Street. I was allowed to go to Sunday school two blocks down the street at St. Paul's Methodist Church, where my paternal grandmother, Francina, was a member.

I attended a private kindergarten, owned by a Mrs. Wright. She was very strict. She would strike our fingers with a ruler or whip us with a bamboo pole if we did not learn our lessons or songs. We were all afraid of her.

My dad finally came home, honorably discharged from the Army, and he found my mom dressing me in those Donald Duck outfits with the long socks. He asked her, "What is this? This boy looks like a sissy." We went to a western store called Ranchland. There he purchased western clothing for me to wear so I would not look like a sissy.

Dad used his G.I. Bill to attend a trade school in Chicago where he learned to repair radios. This was in the late forties, long before television had reached the South. When he returned home, he had a small workspace in the house to work on radios. He also worked at East Coast Grocery, a wholesaler of sorts, where he sold and delivered groceries to local stores.

A few years later, my baby brother, Kenneth, arrived, and then my sister, Terri. One day, we were sitting on a blanket in our back yard with our dad. Two blocks over was a fire and a big cloud of smoke. We heard fire engines heading in that direction. Dad said that it seemed to be at his mother's house. He told me to stay with the younger children and he hurriedly ran toward the fire.

The fire was at his mother's house. He found her standing underneath a mango tree screaming for my cousin, Patsy. She told Dad that Patsy was still in the large, two-story home. She was afraid Patsy would burn to death. Dad ran into the burning house to find her, but she had jumped out of a window on the opposite side of the house. No one had seen her escape. Dad came out of the house choking and coughing. He was about go back inside with the firemen to look for Patsy, but then spotted her standing underneath the mango tree with our grandmother holding her tight. The house burned to the ground. Everything was lost. The fire was started when the kerosene stove on which my grandmother was cooking exploded. The bathroom sinks and bath tubs were the only items of any use that weren't destroyed. My grandparents had bought the house for $500 in the 1920's. It wasn't long before she had a new home, this one made out of concrete blocks.

During our earliest years, we kids watched the iceman, Mr. Oliver, come around in his truck. We could hear him yell

"Ice!" as he drove down the street. We would hide in the bushes and wait for him to park his truck. While he made his deliveries, we would take ice chips from the truck. He was always shooing us away. When people weren't home, they would leave a placard in the front door to indicate how much ice they needed. The blue side had the large numeral "25" on it, and on the red side it read "50." Usually folks who were not at home would also leave some type of treat for the ice man, such as chitterlings or a piece of sweet potato or pecan pie.

It was about 1946 when my parents purchased a new General Electric refrigerator that had a large motor on top. It also made ice cubes in trays. That fascinated me and my brother. We kept peeking inside to see if we could figure out how the ice was made. Mom scolded us for doing it so much that it wasted electricity and kept the food – and ice – from staying cold. Plus the ice couldn't freeze with the door open all the time.

Our first telephone was a dandy. It was not a rotary phone; those didn't reach the South until the mid-fifties. We had a party line, and for you young readers, that meant that we shared a phone line with other families in the neighborhood. If someone had been on the phone too long, tying up the line, it was likely that someone else on the party line would ask them to get off so they could make a call. Because of the party line system, everyone in town knew your business, because a lot of people would be nosy and listen in on other people's conversations. It's amazing what sticks in our brain. I recall our telephone number; it was 967XJ. A couple of years later, we finally got a private line. Our number was 967-J.

I mentioned earlier about some of the old remedies used for colds and whooping cough. Most old folk thought that castor oil and mineral oil could cure anything. In our house, if someone coughed, we all had to take some of this awful "medicine." My mom would take a bottle of castor oil, place it in a pot of boiling water on the stove, and then make us line up to take a big dose from a large spoon. She would have the spoon in one hand and a lemon or an orange segment in the other to help get it down. A spanking paddle would be nearby in case we refused to take it. I used to run down the street to cough so Mom wouldn't hear me and make all of us have to take it. If you have never had to take the stuff, let me tell you that it was even worse when you burped it up.

Adding to the refrigerator and the phone, our house got even more modernized in the late forties when my parents purchased a washer machine. It was really something to see. Not only did it wash clothes, but it had a wringer attached to it. Prior to this, my grandma and my mom would build a fire in our backyard underneath a large steel pot filled with water. When the water started to boil, brown soap and bluing were placed in it. When garments were being washed, my grandma would stir the contents with a long stick like a broom or mop handle. Nearby was a two-sink wash basin. My Mom would use a washboard and brown soap to scrub the contents of the pot in one of the sinks. Afterwards, the clothes were placed in the rinse water in the other sink. I stood on a box, rinsed the garments, and then put them through the wringer, turning it by hand. From there the clothes were be placed in a tin tub and then hung on the clotheslines to dry.

During my early years, I watched my grandma and

mom iron clothes. The ironing board was near the kerosene stove in the kitchen. Six to ten irons were placed atop the stove to get heated. For more than an hour, I used to watch them. When one iron got lukewarm, it would be replaced with a hot one.

Milk was delivered to people's homes in those days. Only white men could get the job as a milkman. No blacks could deliver milk, even in Colored Town. Empty milk bottles would be placed on the front porch with the order and the money inside.

During my early years, we ate a lot of Spam. I always wondered where Spam came from. I decided to get an answer. I went down the street to talk with an old wise woman. She was the daughter of a former slave, and she smoked a corn cob pipe. I asked, "Where does Spam come from?" She took a big puff on that pipe and said, "Spam comes from Spamolopes." I had never heard of a Spamolope, let alone seen one.

My Dad said to me one day, "Come on Son, we're going rabbit hunting."

I asked, "Dad, can we hunt Spamolopes instead? I've never seen one before."

"There's no such thing as a Spamolope!" he told me. I was so disappointed.

Next door to my grandma's house where we lived was my grandma's candy store. There were times when she would ask me to watch the store for a few minutes. I would pretend to not like the idea, but I was glad because I loved the peanut butter candies called "Mary Jane's." I would pocket a couple of pieces each time I was watching the store.

Mrs. Little was a very elderly woman who lived down the street from us and had a milk cow named Molly. Each morning she would walk Molly to the grassy area that bordered the canal. There Molly would graze until the late afternoon. Mrs. Little milked her on a daily basis and sold the milk to locals.

My favorite playmate was Ernest Latimer. He lived three doors from me. Along with other neighborhood kids, we would shoot marbles for fun, and we would listen to the radio to our favorite programs. Some of our favorite radio programs were *Nick Carter, Master Detective, Mr. Keene, Tracer of Lost Persons, Superman, Amos and Andy, Roy Rogers,* and *Jack Benny.*

Ernest was a couple years older than me. He used to take me to the movie matinees on Saturday afternoons. There was a theater located in Colored Town on Avenue D, which was the main street. My grandmother would give the both of us money for admission and snacks. We used to see cowboys like Johnny Mack Brown, Hopalong Cassidy, Roy Rogers, Whip Wilson, John Wayne, and Wild Bill Elliot.

My grandma told Ernest that if he allowed anything to happen to me, she would kill him, and he knew she wasn't kidding. One day when we were in the theater Ernest threw ice from a snow cone and hit a kid on the head. The usher, Leon Knowles, threw him out. I didn't know this and a half-hour later, when Ernest hadn't returned to his seat, I went looking for him, only to learn Mr. Leon had put him out. I went outside and saw Ernest sitting on a box. He told me what had happened, but he was afraid to go home without me because he was afraid my Grandma would kill him. We went home and shot marbles.

Eighth Street, where we lived, was really a busy street. There were a number of businesses and churches on this street. There was a barbershop a few doors down from our house. That is where the locals went to get a haircut and argue about politics, sports, and current events. One guy used to read an almanac prior to going to the barbershop so he could keep up and sound smart.

Mr. Brown had a sundry store on the corner of Eighth Street and Avenue C. People could purchase ice cream, sodas, malts, candy, and over the counter drugs at his store. He used to scold us kids for sliding on his terrazzo floors in our socks. His son, Martin, was very sickly and died at an early age. He was one of our playmates.

Reverend Albert Stone owned one of the local mortuaries, on Seventh Street and Avenue C. His grandson, Samuel, was like an older brother to me and to some of the other kids. Another mortuary was owned and operated by Percy Peek. His wife and daughter tried for years to get me to marry their granddaughter when we would grow up. That never happened.

There were many black businessmen in Colored Town, including shade tree mechanics. Those were the fellows who had no shop; people would have their cars fixed, maybe, just under a tree. There were no computers in those days that could analyze a car's mechanical problems. The mechanic on Eighth Street and Avenue D named Central Richardson would drive a car around the block and listen. When he returned to his garage, he usually knew what the problem was and how to fix it.

Mr. Richardson had nine children. His girls were able to do mechanical work along with his boys. One of the daughters, Sylvia, had tools and sheets of cardboard in the trunk of her car. This was in case she had to work on her own car. It was an old car that had a lot of problems, and she would use the cardboard to lie on while she tool away underneath.

There were several small cafes in Colored Town. For a dollar or two, when I was a little kid, one could get a plate full of food. There were no menus or silverware on the tables. A large poster, in most cafes, was tacked on the wall with large letters; that was what was being served. Most cafes served collard and mustard greens, beef stew, grits, fried fish, bacon, eggs and cornbread. There were certainly no upscale restaurants in our area.

My Uncle Bubba owned the first black motel and nightclub in Colored Town. Blacks, including black celebrities, could not stay at motels or hotels in the white areas because of segregation.

I was very confused when I was a small child, unable to understand why white people could come to Colored Town and have businesses, but black folks could not be seen in the white areas of town – especially at night – let alone that they couldn't have a business there

When I would accompany my Mom shopping downtown, I could not understand why I could not use a restroom. If I had to pee, Mom would take me to the nearest alley way to do so. Once I got a spanking when I was downtown when I made a fuss because I wanted to go into a restaurant to eat. I was almost six years old then.

One day my Mom told me that she was going window shopping downtown, and she took me with her. A white woman was doing likewise and had her little boy with her, too. Both of us boys were staring and smiling at one another. He wanted me to hold the toy he had in his hand. His mom suddenly turned around and said harshly to her son, "Don't you ever let me catch you talking to a nigger." She grabbed him by his hand and left hurriedly.

I can only imagine how my mom felt. I was always asking "why" about things. I asked her why the woman called me a nigger. Mom said, "Don't pay attention to anyone who calls you names. Just pretend you didn't hear them and go about your business."

I never understood why blacks had to enter the downtown theater from the rear and sit in a balcony. Never could we sit on the main floor down below. While growing up, I learned that blacks and whites were not to mingle. Some whites wanted blacks to say "Yes sir" and "Yes ma'am," even to their children. I used to hear older black people speaking to the white children that way, even referring to them as "Mister" and "Miss." I could not imagine calling a six-year-old "Mister" or "Miss." But if you didn't play by the white rules, you could be charged by authorities for having no respect!

I hated to go to the beach because I was so skinny. I recall that it was a bright and sunny day on the Fourth of July in 1951. I had a very large inner tube. My parents did not like the idea of me floating on the tube in the ocean. Maybe for good reason. One time when I was on it the weather changed. Suddenly it started raining really hard and the waves got gigantic. I found myself being pulled away from the shore and out to sea. I called for help, but no one could hear me because the storm was so loud. A large wave knocked me out of the tube and into the current. I had almost given up. I began to swallow the salt water. I was going under. I thought I was done for.

Suddenly I was grabbed by my wrist and pulled to the surface. At first I thought I had drowned and was being brought up by an angel or God. But I was, of course, still alive, and it was a friend of mine, Bernard Shaw, who had been swimming nearby and had seen me get into trouble. He saved my life. My parents had been looking for me through the rain and big waves, and they were most thankful that Bernard had saved me.

My family took a vacation during the summer of 1957. We lived in segregated Florida. My mother's parents lived in (less-segregated) Detroit. Mom told us that we were going to drive there in our '56 Oldsmobile to visit them. This trip would probably take three to four days on the road. We kids were wondering how this trip was going to work. We couldn't eat and sleep in hotels or inns along the way. Mom said," Don't worry, the Lord will make a way somehow."

Before we began our trip, Mom made and packed sandwiches made of cold cuts and soda pop in coolers and put them in the trunk of our car.

It was pretty tough travelling, as my dad spent a lot time trying to find a station that would sell us gasoline. There were times when we could not use the restrooms. We would have to find an area just off the highway to relieve ourselves. My parents would have probably been arrested or harassed by a hate group if we'd been caught. I really felt sorry for my parents because of not being allowed to stay in inns. My dad did most of the driving while my mom slept. Then she would drive a little while Dad slept. We three kids sat and slept in the back seat.

After going through some hard traveling times, things got much easier for us in northern Kentucky. We could buy gas and use restrooms with no problems. What a blessing.

We got to visit our relatives in Detroit for a week and a half, but then had to face the ordeal of returning home. We had transmission problems in Norristown, Tennessee and had to stay over for a couple of days. We had to spend those nights in a boarding house in Colored Town as we could not stay in white owned hotels or inns near the highway. This boarding house was awfully scary and needed a good cleaning. We ate in an old café nearby.

# *Going to School*

I learned very early on that blacks always knew how important education was. I was getting ready to start elementary school. This school was composed of old, dilapidated, single-walled, wooden buildings. There was one two-story building with a long stairway, which led to the second floor. Nothing would have passed today's building codes. Wood stoves were used in the winter for heat. In those days, the white schools had gyms, cafeterias and playgrounds but our school had no cafeteria, gym, or playground.

Still, I was excited about attending the school. I spoke with my grandma about it. She told me that the first school for blacks was located on Eighth Street in what was called by local residents "The Bottom." During the early 1900's, black children wanted to learn to read and write. Old, inadequate, and used materials from the white schools were given to the blacks. My grandma and other black families began a campaign to establish a black school. An old tin building was used for the first black school. This building had been used by the school district to store supplies for the white schools.

My grandma told me that during the early Twenties, there was a school for black students located at Means Court and Thirteenth Street. In those days classes were taught up to the eighth grade. Many of the residents wanted a four-year high school. After a lot of red tape, the school was accredited as a senior high school and was named Lincoln

Park Academy, since its location was in the Lincoln Park district.

The school had no place for basketball games. Grandma and members of the PTA raised money to buy the land for a basketball court. They sold fish and other sandwiches for ten cents. The school board agreed to build a court made of concrete at the corner of Thirteenth and Means Court. Eventually an enclosed tin fence was built by an old carpenter named Johnny Mitchell. I understand that he never missed a game from the twenties to the time of his death. He and my grandma were the best of friends, and I knew him personally. He used to walk with me to school to make certain that I got there safely. He never drove a car. He rode a bicycle that had a large wire basket on the front handlebars containing his tools.

Grandma told me that there were between three and five teachers in those days including the principal. There were no teaching materials; not even a dictionary.

James Espy was the first principal of Lincoln Park School. He requested a dictionary from the district. The superintendent ordered the dictionary. A white principal also requested a dictionary. When Mr. Espy went to pick up the dictionary, the superintendent told him that he had already given it to the white principal. The superintendent told Mr. Espy not bother him any more about a dictionary.

To avoid integrating schools, county politicians redistricted the school district boundaries. As a result, black and white schools were segregated throughout the Jim Crow Era.

I have many memories from the Means Court Elementary School. In 1948, I was in the first grade. Miss Dicey Middleton was my first grade teacher. I was already reading at a first grade level, as I had learned to do so from my kindergarten teacher, Mrs. Wright. I even remember some classmates names; Anne Boatwright, Henry Saulter and Ruby Washington. Mrs. White, who was also from a pioneer family, was my second grade teacher.

In 1950 we moved into a new house built by my dad and Mr. Hall who was a family friend. It was next door to my grandma's house on Dundas Court. It had three bedrooms and one bath and during the winter it was heated by a kerosene stove. Since we were a family of five, it was always a hassle to get to get to use the bathroom.

My third grade teacher was Annette Espy. She was also the choral director at the high school. I was quite the speller in those days. She would give us a list of words to study at the beginning of each week. On Fridays, we had a spelling bee. The first place winner would get a dime and the second place winner would get a nickel. I would get one or the other almost every week. Mrs. Espy also checked to see if we had on clean clothing and had taken a bath.

I remember in the fourth grade my teacher, Miss Long, said that she was going to teach us to crochet. We boys thought that she meant just the girls. But she said that everyone was going to learn, otherwise they would receive an unsatisfactory grade in citizenship. She gave us two days to purchase the materials (a crocheting needle and yarn). Later that afternoon, I walked into our living room. My dad was sitting in his recliner reading a Zane Grey novel. I waited a few moments for him to look up.

Finally I said to him, "Hey Dad, guess what?" He put his novel down in his lap and asked, "What?" I told him what Miss Long had said about teaching us to crochet, otherwise we would get an unsatisfactory grade in citizenship. He replied simply, "Okay." I was really disappointed because he was such a macho man, I thought he would raise some kind of hell about it. I went to my room. Later that day, Dad asked me to repeat what I had said about the crocheting. He said, "No way. You are not crocheting; that's sissy stuff. It's okay if you get an unsatisfactory grade in citizenship." I walked out of the room grinning like a Cheshire Cat.

My fifth grade home room teacher was Mildred Glinton. She was once a former neighbor of ours on Eighth Street. She chose me to perform in my first operetta called "The Inn of the Golden Cheese." At times she would take some of us students to the Bethune-Cookman College in Daytona Beach to see concerts.

I was in the sixth grade in 1954. My teacher was Mrs. Warrick. She was very a light-skinned woman who looked like President George Washington. She also taught my parents back in their school days. She was known to use palmetto rods to whip those who were unruly and for not doing their homework or lessons. We were afraid of her.

One day in 1954 my Mom asked me to come home for lunch instead of eating at school. She said she had a surprise for me. All morning long I was dying with curiosity. I rushed home. Mom had the noontime local news on the radio. A moment or two later, there was a swearing-in ceremony on the air. It was my dad being sworn-in as the first black deputy sheriff in Saint Lucie County. Sheriff Johnny Norvel said that Dad would be able to arrest anyone, regardless of race, color, or creed. Mom and I could not believe what we were hearing. No one ever thought that anything like this would ever happen in our lifetime. As I said, in the Deep South, black city policemen had never been allowed to arrest whites; a white officer had to be called in to make an arrest.

All excited, I went back to school and told my classmates, but they did not believe me.

I was happy for Dad, but it did cause some problems. There was a constant stream of threatening telephone calls to our house from white militants. Dad said that they would have to kill him before he would ever resign.

Deputies in those days wore civilian clothes and carried a .38 caliber Smith & Wesson revolver. They drove their own cars but the county maintained them. The cars had large gold stars on both front doors. Like most of the deputies, Dad's work car was also our family car, so we often got hateful stares from some whites.

Dad had no scheduled shift. He worked 24/7. It was nothing for him to receive a call during the wee hours of the morning; he had to go. He was very seldom at home.

Once he arrested four whites and was transporting them to the county jail. One of them said, "I can't believe we've been arrested by a nigger."

Another day Dad came home for lunch. Afterwards he decided to sit in his recliner to read a few pages of his Zane Grey novel. Moments later two young black women stood at the entrance of our house. They were shouting obscenities at Dad. Just then, an old 82-year-old neighbor woman named Mrs. Sweet was passing by very slowly, as she did all of the time. She was on her way to Mr. Adam's grocery store.

Dad went outside to apprehend them. They ran in different directions. Mrs. Sweet said to Dad, "You get that one; I'll get the other one." Mrs. Sweet chased one woman into an alley and tackled her. Then she slapped her a few times for not being respectful, before bringing her back to my dad. A number of neighbors had seen this because of all the yelling, and no one could believe their eyes because they'd only seen Mrs. Sweet walking at a snail's pace. After delivering the woman to my dad, she went on to Mr. Adam's store as though nothing had happened.

One Saturday night, Dad and his patrol partner, Aaron "Deac" Richardson, were driving down the main street, in Colored Town, when suddenly both back doors to the patrol car opened and two guys jumped in. Dad pulled over and asked, "What is going on?"

One of the guys said, "Please take us to jail now because we have just robbed someone."

"Do you know who you robbed?" Dad asked.

"Yeah, they call him Bacco," the man said, referring to a mean black cowboy whose nickname was Bacco. No one ever wanted to fight with him, but the panicky guy in the back seat claimed that they had robbed him in a nearby alley. Both said that they had heard of Bacco and his reputation, but never met him in person until that night. They didn't know who he was when they were robbing him, or they wouldn't have.

Then Bacco came over to the police car and told Dad and Deac that he had just been robbed. The suspects in the back seat pleaded with Dad not to let Bacco get them. That's when Bacco saw the two guys in the back seat of the patrol car. He told Dad, "Those are the two guys who robbed me." And to the men in the back, Bacco said, "I will see you guys again one of these days." Both were incarcerated for armed robbery. I don't know if they ever ran into Bacco again.

Another night Dad and Deac were in pursuit of a '54 Lincoln coupe that was exceeding the speed limit on a main street. Suddenly, the car made a sharp right turn, and Dad saw a body roll out onto the pavement. It looked like the driver had struck a pedestrian. Dad's partner got out to check the injured person. Dad chased after the driver.

Suddenly, the car crashed into a house. Dad thought

that the driver must be seriously injured, but when he got out to investigate he discovered that there was no one in the car. It turned out that the driver had made such a sharp right turn he'd thrown himself out of the car. He was the man laying in the street.

In 1954, I graduated elementary school at Means Court and was scheduled to become a student at the new school on Seventeenth Street. Though I lived a few blocks from the white school, maybe a fifteen minute walk, because of segregation I had to instead walk three miles to our new school. I didn't mind, as I was used to segregation and never thought that the white man would ever allow us to get ahead.

Our new school was really nice. There was a real gymnasium. No more playing basketball on an outside concrete court enclosed by a tin fence. There were showers with hot water and locker rooms. There were even flushing toilets. Real country boys thought these toilets were something. Most of them had only used outdoor toilets where pattern papers, newspapers, Sears, Penney's and Montgomery Ward catalogues were used, instead of regular toilet tissue.

I recall once when I was still new to the school, I had to use the restroom in a hurry. I rushed inside and was attacked by a group of girls who chased me out, calling me a pervert. When I got outside, I noticed pranksters had taken the "WO" from the sign on the door, leaving only the word MEN.

Also about our new school, though there were several black owned businesses, none sponsored a Little League baseball team or a Pop Warner football team like the whites had.

Another thing, we enjoyed our new cafeteria; lunch was

thirty cents. It was there that I had gingerbread for the first time in my life.

I had an after-school job delivering newspapers. It was tough, because most of the roads in Colored Town were just plain dirt. When it rained, it was hard to pedal a bicycle in the thick mud. Every other month, a grader would come to scrape the roads. There was never a problem like this in the white areas of town.

Both black and white paperboys had to go to the circulation department in downtown Fort Pierce to get our newspapers. We did not mingle. We had access to tables to fold the papers, put them in our bags and go out to deliver. Blacks wanted to have zones, rather than have a customer here and there on the other side of town, but the whites liked what they had so their way prevailed.

When I finished delivering papers, I would maybe get home dog-tired, and try to study for school. It was an unrewarding job. Most of the time, the customer would claim they had no money. But they were still the ones to complain if they did not get a paper. Also, when it rained, the paper, like the mail, had to be delivered.

To make things worse, I hated the people who were in charge of the newspaper. They were outright racists. They would report only one page of news about blacks, and only on Sundays, and they titled the page "Colored News."

There was a man named Charles Bolden who wrote the black news for the racist owners. He was also in charge of black delivery boys. The only time blacks could make headlines was if they committed a crime. Mr. Bolden was seriously thinking of publishing his own newspaper. I told him I would work for him, if he decided to follow through.

As it happened, Mr. Bolden managed to find antiquated

printing equipment and a Linotype machine to put out a paper which was called The Chronicle. It was my job to pour the liquid lead for the Linotype. I also operated the printing presses by hand, repaired the motors that operated the newspaper machine, and made certain there was enough ink to print. Each sheet of the newspaper was fed into the machine by hand.

Copies of the paper were taken to the post office and the Greyhound bus station on Thursday nights, as there were customers outside our county. The reporters did a good job of reporting the news in the colored communities here and in our neighboring counties. This paper was a success.

While in Lincoln Park Academy Junior High School, I sang with the school's chorus. I had a very high tenor voice and I was almost a soprano. My dad would have wanted me to become a sports jock, but I was just too small. Sadly, neither he nor my mom attended the musicals, even though I often had solo parts.

My grandma was a piano teacher. She wanted to teach me to play. Foolishly I refused because my friends said that it would make me become a sissy. She told me that I would be sorry someday because I refused to learn to play. She was so right.

I spent a lot of time listening to classical music, as that is all we heard at our house. We never played gospel or spirituals in our house which is what I heard in many black homes, and to this day, I only know the first verse of "Amazing Grace."

On the radio, I would hear some of my favorite singers: Doris Day, Rosemary Clooney, Mario Lanza, Howard Keel, Jeanette McDonald, Nelson Eddy and Gordon McCrae among others. I used to say, "I'm going to sing with some of them, someday." My friends used to laugh at me, because I talked like I was white with dreams like that. They said that would never happen, not in a million years, because I was colored.

Throughout school, my grades were only average. The reason was that I spent too much time getting into mischief and not studying. My dad said that I was embarrassing the family by getting into trouble, especially with him being a deputy. Most of the people in my hometown, including my relatives, never thought that I would ever amount to anything. One day he and the sheriff (his boss) had a discussion about me. The sheriff asked Dad to let him have me the coming summer to work on the ranch.

# *Growing Up*

Summer came along and school was out. Dad again took me to the Ranchland western store. There he bought me two pairs of western jeans, some shirts, a hat, and boots. I had no idea why he was buying this attire for me. I knew if my buddies saw me wearing this unstylish crap – that's what I thought of these clothes – they would laugh at me. I had no clue as to what was about to happen.

A couple of mornings later, at about 4:30, my Dad woke me up and said, "Get up and put on those jeans and a shirt." I asked him, "What's going on?" He said, "You're going to work on the sheriff's ranch for a while so hurry up." He said the foreman, Charlie Chavis, was coming to pick me up in his Jeep pickup truck in a few minutes.

Charlie arrived shortly afterwards and picked me up. I was very excited. I could not believe I was going to work on a ranch. After a long drive, we finally arrived at the ranch. Charlie told me what was expected of me. He showed me how to feed the horses, and check and clean their hooves. Initially I was very afraid of the horses. But it wasn't long before I was used to them, and my fear of horses was gone.

There were no horse trailers on the ranch. Instead, axle-wide holes were dug into the ground and large trucks with side rails were backed into them. Then the horses were walked onto the bed of the truck and tied to ropes. The back gates of the trucks were secured and off they'd drive out of the holes.

I went on my first cattle drive along with the sheriff's

daughter, Ann, Maggie Carlton, Charlie, and some other cowboys. We drove the cattle down a country road onto an area that had a large corral. All of the cows were checked for screw worms and sprayed for certain insects.

It was a great experience, but I was bothered somewhat at chow time. Charlie and I were the only blacks there and we could not sit with the rest of the crew to eat lunch. I was not surprised about not being able to join them as I knew that was the southern way of life. But it still made me feel like I was nobody.

Another time at the ranch, Charlie and I loaded the Jeep pickup with fence posts and barbed wire. We had to build miles of fence near the turnpike. If we should run out of fence posts, we would cut down a pine tree, measure the posts with axe handles, cut them up, and use them for posts. It's extremely hot and humid in Florida in the summer so I worked most of the time without a shirt. One day, my wire stretchers broke. I had to use a claw hammer to pull and hold the barbed wire in place with my legs, while I stapled it with another hammer.

Suddenly I looked up and saw that the wire had come undone and was heading my way. I tried to run, but the wire caught up with and wrapped around me, causing several cuts and bruises. Charlie had to cut me free with his wire cutters.

At times, Charlie and I also had chores to do around the ranch. I didn't like being around the ranch people. Charlie told me just do my work and not initiate any conversations with anyone, because no one there liked black people. It bothered me when folk I had worked with walked passed by me without speaking. It also bothered me being served lunch on a tin tray, just like the ones they used to serve prisoners in the jail. Sometimes I wondered if I was getting more sensitive, and maybe too angry.

Working on the ranch was a good experience but it did not last very long. Afterwards, I worked with my next door neighbor, Brit Stockton, who was a labor contractor. We would pick up field workers between five and six in the morning in a '51 Dodge bus, and transport them to the tomato fields at various locations. Wages were God-awful. Men were paid seven dollars a day and women five; we were always paid in cash. For those doing piece work, it was ten cents for each wire basket full of tomatoes.

There was always a poor white overseer watching the laborers. This one we had was so poor he didn't even have a watch. He would look up at the sun to tell the time, and actually he was pretty accurate most of the time.

I hated every moment being in the field. We did not have portable toilets or fresh drinking water. There was a boy carrying a galvanized bucket with a dipper. In it was sulphur-tainted water that smelled like rotten eggs and tasted awful.

My job was to drive to different areas of the field to pick up loaded boxes. One day as I was driving a company truck slowly through the fields, the boss's daughter suddenly jumped into the cab with me. She was white, blonde, quite pretty, and only about 19 years old. I was deathly afraid because blacks had been known to be tortured and lynched for even being near a white woman. I asked her in a nice way to get out. She said, "I just want to ride for a while." I told her that I didn't want any problems with her father. She said, "Oh he won't mind."

I saw her dad from a distance and drove up to where he was standing in the field. I got out and said to him, "Sir, your daughter got into the truck with me; I asked her to get out, because I didn't want any problems with you." He said, "Let her ride with you if she wants to. I don't mind."

I was shocked. She was standing nearby grinning like a jack-o-lantern. She said, "I told you so; let's get back to the truck." I was shaking the rest of the day, as she was constantly pinching me and laughing at me.

I was driving a lot through Indian River County and had good reason to be nervous. The sheriff there was a man named Osteen. He did not like black people at all. He was known for making blacks stick their heads into the driver's window. He would then roll up the window on their necks and then drive down the road a ways to watch them run sideways and listen to them gag. Most were seriously injured, but no one in those days would listen to a black person's complaint.

Indian River County was adjacent to Saint Lucie County. I was told by some black residents of that county, that Osteen used to use a blackjack or a small bat to beat black folk. Most of the time he lacked evidence when he arrested a black for a crime, but frequently, blacks would serve quite a spell in his jail for a crime they did not commit. And this was the county where the tomato fields were located and where I was working.

Black residents tolerated Osteen for many years; most were not registered voters. Then one day the sheriff died. To this day I still do not know whether it was a natural death or if he was killed by someone. I do know for a fact that the black residents of that county celebrated his death for more than a week. His family was sad, but blacks were very happy. There were so many barbecues and fish frys that week!

I worked for my dad driving his truck-tractor. He paid a man to teach me the basics, parking and driving. It was fun, but hard work.

A short time later, I was transporting citrus to the different juice plants on the west coast of Florida. Near one of the plants was the headquarters of the Ku Klux Klan. I did not know that until much later. I was in that area during the wee hours of the morning.

After the citrus was delivered, the culls (the peels) were placed on the trailer to take and dump at a nearby cattle ranch. Supposedly, the cattle produced better milk after eating these peels.

Early one morning about three, I had just dropped off a trailer load of culls to some cattle. As I was leaving, I heard a loud popping sound. I got out, checked the tires on the trailer, and saw that an inside rear tire had blown. I pulled off the road into a turnout. This was my worst nightmare. I was afraid that I would be confronted by members of the Ku Klux Klan.

I was in the process of changing the trailer tire in the darkness when a law enforcement officer driving by saw me and stopped. He asked, "What are you doing, Boy"?

I don't know why, I guess it was my nature, but I was smart to him and said, " I'm eating breakfast."

He got out of his patrol car and asked, "Did you steal this rig?"

I told him, "This rig belongs to my father and me. I have all of the necessary paperwork in the glove compartment." He told me to show him, and I got out the paperwork. He told me to read it to him, probably to see if I could really read. I had wised up and was careful not to say anything more that was sarcastic. I mean, he had a gun. In those days in the Deep South, he could shoot me and say that I tried to attack him. It would have been justifiable homicide.

Another time, an autocar truck tractor rig I was driving blew an engine on the turnpike near Fort Pierce. It was a 55-foot trailer loaded with chicken feed that I was transporting to Gainesville, Georgia; the site of another Ku Klux Klan headquarters. I asked, "Why me?" There was no answer, but everything worked out.

Yet another early morning, I was in Athens, Georgia trying to find the truck stop. I asked a white man for directions. I think he purposely gave me the wrong directions. I drove through a white residential area, which was forbidden for coloreds. I was pulled over by a white policeman, who said, "Where in the hell do you think you're going, Boy?"

I explained to him that I was lost, and I needed to buy fuel for my truck. Could he tell me where I could find a truck stop. He threatened to put me in jail, but he let me go, but without giving me directions.

I finally found the truck stop. It was dark and rainy as I pulled in. I rolled down my window and asked a white attendant to fill up my tanks. He had blonde hair and wore thick prescription glasses. He said, "Sorry, boy, but I can't help you." When I asked him why not, he said he would lose his job if he were caught helping a colored man fuel.

I said, "It's dark and so no one can see me, here in my truck, and I'm paying cash."

He replied, "These fuel tanks are for whites. There are tanks in back for coloreds."

I drove in the back. Sure enough, there was a black attendant there pumping fuel for black truckers. Black truckers could not eat in the restaurant nor sleep in the facilities there. Instead, the black trucker could order a sandwich or hot dog through the kitchen window and pay the cook with cash. This was the way of life in those days, in the Deep South.

It being Florida, we had window screens in our house. They could be opened by unhooking two fasteners at the bottom and pushing the screen outward. My dad was very strict about me being home by eleven o'clock at night. When he would come home from work at night, he would check my bedroom to see if I was in bed. A few minutes later, I would listen to hear his bedroom door shut. Then I knew he was going to sleep. I would wait for a few more minutes, then I would sneak out of that window and join my friends who were waiting for me down the street. I had been doing this for a long time. There were times when I would push my mom's DeSoto sedan from our garage and out to the street with the help of my friends.

When I returned later I would speed up on Tenth Street, shut off the ignition, turn into our driveway, and coast quietly into the carport. Then I would open the screen, climb inside, get out of my clothes, and get into bed. There were never any problems doing this until this one night when I tried to open the screen, and I found that I couldn't get in. It had been nailed shut. Apparently, my dad was aware of my scheme, probably for a long time, and he had nailed the screen shut.

I went to the front door and knocked repeatedly because it was cold. Through the window I saw my dog resting beside the heater. I knocked again. My dad shouted back at me, "Don't knock, because you don't live here anymore."

I walked down to the part of town where the homeless guys hung out, underneath a Mulberry tree, standing over a 55-gallon drum with a fire in it. One of them asked, "Aren't you the high sheriff's son?"

I replied, "No. He and I do look alike, but I'm not him."

After about an hour, I went back home and through the door promised I'd behave. My mother talked my dad into letting me come inside again. I got a good verbal thrashing from Dad.

Another time I might have gotten into trouble was during lunch time at school. My buddy, Harold "Hoggie" Richardson, and I decided we were going to steal a pan of meatloaf from the cafeteria. I saw one near the window where the empty trays were dropped off. I also saw that the dishwasher was not there. So I went through the window with Hoggie holding me by my feet. The plan was for him to pull me out fast as soon as I grabbed the pan.

Suddenly, just as I grabbed the pan, it became very dark. A tornado was headed toward the school and it had blocked out the sun. Of course we had to abort the plan. Fortunately, the tornado turned away from the school, so we were okay, but it tore up a few churches, homes, and part of the downtown area. On the southeast coast of Florida, there were no basements or any kind of shelters that protected us from tornados. Not that we were in a position to take cover.

Speaking of the cafeteria, I was blamed for a different incident that really did occur there. It had nothing to do with me, but it shows you the kind of reputation I'd earned. It seemed someone had placed a large sea turtle in the cafeteria early one morning. The principal called my name over the PA system and asked that I come to the central office immediately. When I arrived at his office, he told me about the sea turtle in the cafeteria and said that this was my method of operation. I told him that I had nothing to do with it, but he did not believe me. However, I did not get a suspension because there was no proof that I was involved.

I later learned that the turtle had come ashore to lay her eggs. Afterwards, she was turned upside down and placed on the bed of a pickup truck and brought to the school early that morning. The turtle was placed by the exit door, and it had crawled around until it had found its way to the kitchen. Personnel there were standing atop of the steam tables and screaming. The custodian saw what was happening and called the SPCA, who sent people over to remove the turtle.

A friend of mine who was a senior at school was about to graduate and asked if I would be interested in taking over his after-school job at the public library downtown. The scenery was beautiful outside, as it overlooked the Indian River (Intercostal Waterway). I thought it might be a good place to work, so I was introduced to Mrs. Parsons, the head librarian. She interviewed me and I got the job.

I worked at the library as a janitor from four in the afternoon until ten at night, Monday through Friday. There were no other blacks employed there, nor did they allow black students to use the library. They used white high school students to assist the librarians.

I never said anything but I hated working there because everyone treated me like I was trash. But the fact was that I needed the job. If someone dropped something and I was nearby, I was expected to pick it up. Otherwise, I was ignored, which was fine with me. I didn't want any problems anyway. I didn't want to get killed like Emmett Till did, for allegedly flirting with at a white woman in Mississippi in 1955. (I had seen a picture of him in the Pittsburgh Courier, an all-black newspaper that my grandma distributed.)

Colored Town was about two miles from downtown. I had to walk home each night, and I was afraid that I might to run into some kind of trouble. Every other night there were carloads of white kids driving by yelling obscenities at me.

I also had problems with a white girl who drove a green '51 Ford. She would be waiting for me at different areas on the route I took to walk home. Every other night she would drive slowly beside me as I walked and asked would I like have a ride. I pleaded with her to please leave me alone. I tried taking alternative routes home, but she seemed to find me anyway.

During this time, it was nothing to hear of a black person lynched for no reason at all. While walking home at night, I would think if I was caught even just talking to that white girl, I could get lynched. I didn't know but maybe she was trying to set me up. It was scary.

The students at my school asked if they could use the library. After all, their parents were taxpayers and they should be able to use it. The next day, I spoke with the head librarian about the request. She sat at her desk with a pencil in her mouth. I guess she was thinking because she didn't say anything; she just stared at me. I could tell she was very upset. Finally she said, "Well, only two can come, if they don't come to play."

I said, "We have themes and essays like the white students."

She let me know in so many words that she thought I was making too many waves. Two black students did come to the library to do research. When whites complained to the head librarian, the blacks were barred from coming to the library anymore.

I had worked there for about a year when this

happened, and it wasn't long afterward that I came to work one afternoon and saw a black woman I knew to be a very reputable housekeeper being interviewed by Mrs. Parsons. I had a gut feeling that she was going to replace me, and sure enough, before long, I was fired.

In 1959, my dad leased a Phillips 66 Service station at the corner of 25th Street and Avenue D in Fort Pierce. I worked there every day after school. Gasoline then was about 24 cents a gallon.

I remember the first car tire I repaired. It was on a '50 Buick sedan. After repairing it, I went around to the front of the station to pump gas for a customer. I knew that I had put too much air in the tire, and I rushed back to let some out. But by the time I got back there, the tire was gone! I could not figure out what had happened to it. Just then I heard a loud explosion down the street. A few minutes later, the owner of the Buick and his friends returned to the station, on foot, and covered with dust. The tire had exploded in the trunk of their car. The back window had been shattered, the rear doors wouldn't shut right, the back seat was damaged, the chrome had come lose, and the trunk could no longer lock. The owner admitted having taken the tire because he didn't want to have to pay for it. Had he paid for the tire, I would have been in deep trouble.

One night, about 10 o'clock, I closed the service station, washed up, and put on a clean-starched Phillips 66 uniform. I drove my jalopy to a favorite spot called Jake's Drive-In. That was where my friends hung out and told lies. While talking to the guys, they saw a beautiful woman standing at the corner of the building, looking at me like she wanted something. One of the guys said, "I think she is trying to get your attention."

I looked and saw her beckoning for me to come to her. I was reluctant because I did not have a clue who she was. The boys were pushing me towards her. Yeah, she was a beauty and somewhat older. She asked me to come to her; said she wanted to talk to me, one on one. I was a bit nervous, but I left my friends and walked around the corner of the building to talk to her.

I noticed that she had her hand in this large handbag. When she asked me if I was I the high sheriff's son, I told her I was. She said that my dad had arrested her a number of times, and she wanted to get even with him. I told her that she should discuss the matter with him. I started to walk away from her, but then I heard behind me, "If you take another step, I will kill you."

She told me who she was and I recognized her name. I won't mention it because she is still alive, but I was suddenly very scared. She had a reputation of doing bodily harm to people. She told me to walk ahead of her to the apartment building across the street. She said,"If you try to run, I will shoot you." I complied because I believed she would.

We arrived at her apartment on the second floor of this building. The door was unlocked. She told me to go inside and sit on the edge of her bed. She told me that she had started to shoot me earlier as she wanted to get even with my Dad. But then she said that she had other plans for me.

I was sitting on the edge of the bed, she was standing a few feet away with a small revolver pointed right at my face. She reached forward and slapped me, and said, "I'm going to make a man out of you."

She asked, "Have you ever made love to a woman before?"

I shook my head.

As she was talking to me, she was undressing. The skirt she was wearing had a row of buttons on it. When she snatched off the skirt, the buttons flew everywhere. She stood there in her panties and bra, still with that pistol aiming at my face.

She told me to take off my clothes. I was very skinny and embarrassed to do so. I had never made love to a woman before. Nor for that matter had I ever seen a nude female. She told me to stop stalling and to get into the bed. I covered myself with the sheet.

She told me what to do. Moments later, she passed out, still holding the gun in her hand. I got out of the bed, put my clothes on, and left as fast as I could without making any noise. In the hallway I saw the manager of the building. She was someone I knew her personally. I explained to her what had occurred and asked that she check on the woman. She told me not to worry, assuring me that everything would be okay. In fact, I saw that woman again. She apologized for the threats she had made, promising that she wouldn't kill me.

I worked for my dad at the service station for the next two years. Then he sold it to a friend and I worked for him as well. I continued working at the station after school and on weekends.

My dad bought me an old '39 Plymouth to use at the station. The body and the doors had been removed; it had no windshield. No girls would ride in it because they didn't want to tear their stockings and get bugs in their face. The Ford Skyliner was a popular car in those days (1958-59). They had removable hardtops. A few of the guys had those cars, and they had the girls.

Because I had no windshield I went to the Army and

Navy store and bought goggles and helmets. When those big Florida bugs get into your mouth, they taste pretty bad. At least the goggles kept the bugs out of my eyes.

Underneath the glove box was a large canister that contained a mixture of bulk oil and other chemicals. It could be opened with a valve. When it was open and I depressed the accelerator, the chemicals would come out through the tailpipe and spray for mosquitoes.

I also had a T-model coil attached underneath the hood, and a chain that was grounded. Whenever I would get out of the car, I would pull a toggle switch. If someone would so much as leaned on my car, they would get a good shock.

I was not allowed to park my car on the Lincoln Park Academy campus, because the principal said it was an embarrassment. One day I was driving my old car. I had my German Shepherd riding along. I turned a corner really sharp, near a ravine. A moment later, I looked back to discover that my dog was not in the car. I back-tracked and saw the dog climbing up the embankment, soaking wet but not injured. Just then, Dad pulled up in his patrol car and asked what happened. I told him. He said that it would not have happened, if I had not been speeding. Later, when he came home, he put two hands full around my neck to express his considerable frustration with me.

There was a chiropractor who lived across from our service station. His family and mine were very close." Doc" was always broke. So broke he would borrow money from me and my brother. Back then, even though gasoline was only about a quarter a gallon, he would only put a half-dollar's worth of gas in his '55 Chrysler, and do that every other day.

He also had a '59 Cadillac coupe which he thought was

going to be a classic someday. He decided to paint it himself. He used a paint brush to paint the bottom brown, using some paint he found in the back of his garage. The top he painted white. He told me that he had gotten a deal on four tires. I asked, "Why did you buy tires from someone other than me?"

He said, "I got 'em for five dollars."

I asked, "Five dollars each?"

"No, I got all four for five bucks," he told me.

I looked at the tires; they were all different sizes and they had almost no tread. I asked Doc if he was trying to commit suicide!

The floor of his car was made of 3/8-inch plywood. There were large holes in the floor through which you could see the ground.

One sunny day, as Doc was driving down in town, he saw a beautiful woman walking down the street. His intentions were to stop to offer her a ride. He stepped on the brake pedal, but his foot slipped from the pedal and his foot and leg went through the hole in the plywood. He burned his leg on the muffler and his foot was dragging on the pavement. Then his shoe hit a manhole cover, knocking off the heel of his shoe. He somehow managed to stop the car and pull it over to the side of the street. He got out and retrieved the heel of his shoe. Then he opened the trunk and got out his jack handle. Then he sat on the edge of the trunk and tried to replace the heel, holding the shoe in one hand, and smacking the heel with other. He said it would be too expensive to take the shoe to a cobbler.

One really rainy day, Doc had his mother in the car. He drove through a large mud puddle and muddy water up came through the plywood and soaked his mom. As she was wiping the water from her face, she said, "Son, why don't you go to the Cadillac dealership and buy a new car. I'll make the down payment for you. You're going kill yourself in this piece of junk."

The next day, Doc went to the dealership. He finally chose a decent car. The salesman asked him to drive his old car around to the back of the lot so that no one would see it. Doc said, "She's yours now. You drive her where you want her to be." The salesman got in the car, very perturbed, and drove the car around to the back. He got even more upset when his foot slipped from the pedal, and his leg went through the hole and got burned by the hot muffler.

Doc's dad passed away, and at the gravesite after his funeral, the family asked for the casket to be opened again, so they could take a last look. When it was opened, some members of the family threw cash money into the casket. Most of the family were professionals. One of the brothers was a soldier. They told him that he didn't have to put anything in the casket because soldiers didn't make very much money. He said he wanted to contribute also so he wrote a check for $1,200 and tossed it into the casket. He was the last one to leave the gravesite, staying there until Doc's dad was buried, to make sure no one got their hands on that check. Each month when he received his bank statements, he was always afraid that check would appear.

# *College Years*

In my last year of high school, I was a member of the school's chorus. Earl Little was the choral director. He arranged a trip for the group to hear the chorus from Florida A&M University. This concert was being held at Attucks High School in Fort Lauderdale. I was so impressed with the sound of those voices. Most of all, I saw the girl of my dreams performing with the group. My mind was made up. I decided to become a student there. Maybe then I could meet her in person.

In the fall of 1960, I enrolled at Florida A&M in Tallahassee. My dad was insisting that I become a physician. He thought he could tell me what I was going to do since he and Mom were financing my education. While I knew that I didn't have the brains to become a doctor, I thought I should at least give it a shot.

Part of my plan worked anyway, because I finally met the girl of my dreams. She was never interested in me as a boyfriend but we became good friends. Still, I gave it a good try. Too good a try, maybe, because I was so blown away by her that I didn't study much. I even skipped classes from time to time. That doesn't cut it for someone who says he's pre-med.

I lived downhill from the university on South Boulevard Street, with two roommates, William Keith and William Taylor. We were from the same hometown and had attended the same high school. We had another roommate, Charles

Harris, who was from a nearby town. Our landlady, Miss Lewis, was a tennis instructor at the university. We had two bedrooms with bunks and a bathroom.

There was no such thing as a microwave oven in those days, but Keith had a hot plate. He would put everything that was edible in one pot. For instance, if he had grits, a can of salmon and some beans, he would put it all in a pot and cook it together. He'd eat anything.

Just prior to the second semester, Mrs. Steele, our choral director said that I should become a music major. I was always thinking that, but knew my parents would not approve. The first semester, my grades were terrible. But in the second semester, I got my grades up to average because I changed my major to business administration. Still, I was on probation. My dad came to the campus and read me the riot act, but he knew I would never be a doctor.

That summer, I worked at a fish market with a buddy, Charlie Bell, who was an apprentice brick mason. The market was owned by a nice elderly white couple. We cleaned and sold fresh fish there.

The following fall semester, I was didn't have the money to return to FAMU. I enrolled instead at Lincoln Junior College, a local institution in my hometown. I was very disappointed. I really wanted to study dramatic arts. But in those days, there were very few black actors, and I didn't think that I would have a chance, being black, trying to pursue an acting career.

While in college, I managed to get a new job at a local pharmacy in my hometown. I did not have a car in those days. I walked for miles to work every day after school. My salary was $42 dollars a week. I delivered medicine and did the janitorial duties there.

The pharmacist who owned the business was intoxicated most of the time. Otherwise, he was an okay guy. However, the pharmacist's wife and the accountant for the business were extremely prejudiced. They did not care for Jews, Asians, or blacks. The wife was always yelling at me, even in the presence of customers. She especially did not like me talking to Jews. She never hired anyone of color as clerks or any other position.

One night, a New York Jewish couple vacationing in Fort Pierce came into the pharmacy. They were returning to New York the next day. He was a doctor. He said, "Young man, when we walked in, she was saying some horrible things to you. Why do you put up with this nonsense?"

I shrugged my shoulders and said, "What can I say?"

He asked "Why don't you come to New York and live with us? There is just too much prejudice here." I thanked them, but didn't accept their offer. He gave me his business card in case I changed my mind.

After they left, my boss asked me, "Why were you talking to those Jews so long? Don't ever let me see you talking to Jews anymore."

I hated every day I had to work there.

To make deliveries, the pharmacy provided me with a two-door Nash-Rambler coupe. Whenever I had to transport my boss (Mrs. "B"), she would sit in the back seat. Her bookkeeper did likewise. Of course, this was the way of life in the Deep South. It made me feel as if I was second class. Her husband (Mr."B") always rode in the front with me.

The clerks at the pharmacy were part time workers who had other professions. Most were very nice to me. Two of the clerks, Tommy Flowers and Michael Moody, always treated me with respect. They were important to me realizing that not all white people were bad to blacks. Tom's Father, W. D. Flowers, wanted to finance my college education, but I was afraid to accept the offer. Besides, I still wanted to study dramatic arts, and that didn't look like a serious idea to my dad or to anyone else.

There were two other pharmacists, Dan Howell and Charlie Justice. Both were very liberal. We enjoyed working together. There were times when they would accompany me to Colored Town. We would have coffee or a bite to eat in a small café. It was a first for them as they had never been around black people before.

The pharmacy did not have a coffee urn. I had to walk across U.S. Highway One to a restaurant to get coffee for the staff. Like every place else, it was segregated. I was not allowed to enter through the front entrance. Instead, I had to enter from the back to go into the kitchen and wait for someone to bring the cups of coffee to me. I had a list of coffees the pharmacy staff wanted. Some of them wanted sugar in their coffee, some wanted cream, and some just plain. If the orders weren't right, I would to go back to the restaurant to get the correct order. Some of the restaurant personnel were very rude to me.

I had the same experience walking home from work at the pharmacy as I did when I worked at the public library when I was in high school. White groups used to follow and harass me, making threats to hang me or just calling me names. I had never heard the names "porch monkey" or "jungle bunny" before. I was too afraid – and too smart – to ask what they meant.

There was a large park that bordered Colored Town. Blacks could walk through there, but were not allowed to have functions or picnics there. One night a group of blacks was returning home from a downtown movie. As they were walking through the park they were attacked by a group of whites. The white policemen released the white group immediately. They transported the blacks to a nearby jail where they were "interrogated" – which means roughed up – before they were released.

Each night after work at the pharmacy, I would feel relieved once I reached Colored Town. I would stop in at a hangout called the "Grill." It was owned by an obese but articulate black man called "Big Joe." Some pretty tough homeboys hung out there. Big Joe was known for getting a Hawksbill knife or a pistol out of his pocket in a flash. I asked him to teach me how to master this technique as I was nervous when I walked at night through White Town. He agreed and I became really fast showing a weapon. In fact, I got so fast that I earned the respect of some of the local blacks who had once bullied me.

I had an old raggedy .22 caliber pistol; the stock was wrapped in black electrical tape. I could pull two knives from my pockets simultaneously, within two seconds. There were times when I would have someone toss an apple or an orange towards me and I would cut them in mid-air. My dad, the deputy sheriff, detested Joe, calling him a thug, but Joe was good to a lot of kids.

One evening, while I was walking from work in White Town, a car with four white males stopped. They got out and began walking towards me. One said, "It's going to be a lot of fun kicking your black ass."

When they got close, I pulled out both my knives and started swinging and gave chase. They ran in all different directions from where their car was. I quickly opened the hood, removed a couple of spark plug wires, tossed them into the bushes nearby, and then ran as fast as I could towards Colored Town. I hid for a while near the Stone Brothers Funeral Home, a black-owned business, to make sure they weren't following me, on foot.

Another night I was walking home through White Town and a white man started following me. He said, "I always wanted to maim me a nigger." He reached into his pocket to get a switchblade knife. I quickly grabbed his wrist and had my own knife at his throat so fast I surprised myself.

I told him, "I will kill you so fast you'll stink standing up." He pleaded for his life. I had no intention of killing him. I pushed him away, and we both ran in opposite directions. From then on, I decided I would take a different route home at night.

One night, I made a delivery to the home of a very beautiful white woman. She had me wait at her front door while she got the money for the prescription. When she returned, she asked what time did I get got off work. I asked her why she wanted to know. She said she wanted me to have a drink with her. I did not say another word to her. I left hurriedly in my delivery car. I was scared, thinking again what happened to Emmett Till. I told one of the pharmacists about what happened, and he said I'd been smart to get out of there fast.

As time passed, my luck worsened. I was getting speeding tickets constantly, I couldn't get a raise in salary, I lost my favorite girlfriend, and wound up not having enough credits to graduate junior college. I was depressed most of the time because I was away from my mom even though we lived in the same town. The war in Vietnam was heating up, and I was thinking of joining the Marines.

In May of 1963, I was involved in a fight at a favorite

hangout on the outskirts of town. I was arrested and jailed. Dan Howell bailed me out, as always. He was very special to me. Each time I had to appear in court, the judge would try my case in his chambers. This was because my dad was a deputy.

I was constantly thinking of leaving the South, because life was just too hard for a black person. Charlie Justice said he was going on vacation and had plans to drive to his hometown in Ada, Ohio. He said that I was welcome to ride with him that far, even though in those days blacks and whites did not travel together. I figured that since I had family in Detroit, maybe I could go there to get a job at one of the automotive plants. Charlie said that he would take me to Lima, Ohio, and from there, I could catch a Greyhound bus to Detroit.

I gave my two-week notice to the pharmacy. I was leery about travelling with Charlie to the North, because it could be dangerous traveling through the South. We could be lynched or burned to death – both of us – just for being in the same car. Yes, it was that bad back then. I told Charlie that I would not be able to eat in any restaurants along the way nor could I stay in any inns or motels. He said, "Don't worry, we'll be fine."

I really hated leaving my mom. My dad would not allow me to see her before I left. He was always putting me out because he thought I was a thug and I probably was then. I sneaked in anyway and saw her. My dad asked if I had any money, and I told him that I had plenty. I was lying; I had less than a hundred dollars.

A few days later, we were off to the North in Charlie's Ford Falcon coupe. We got an awful lot of hateful stares, but it didn't bother him at all. I was the one who was bothered. When Charlie drove, I sat in the back. He sat in the back when I drove. We gassed up where there were colored and white restrooms. If we bought gas at night, I would cover myself on the floor in the back of the car.

We slept in the car in wooded areas just off the highway. Because I couldn't eat in restaurants along the way, Charlie would go in and buy sandwiches and soda pop. Then we would go in to a turnout off the highway and eat hurriedly. We also had to relieve ourselves along the highway in the bushes. I felt so sorry for Charlie; because of me he had to cope with this segregation crap, too.

Whenever we did stop and someone was curious about why we were together, I would tell them that he was my boss, and he was taking me to another one of his farms to do labor.

The trip lasted about four days and I was relieved when around dusk, we finally arrived in Lima, Ohio. Conditions there were much better than in the South. Charlie and I had a bite to eat at the Greyhound bus station, and I purchased a bus ticket for Detroit. A short time later, Charlie and I hugged each other and shook hands. He wished me luck and asked me to visit him if I should return to the South. As I watched him drive off, he put his arm out of the window and waved goodbye to me. A moment later, he was gone.

Suddenly I felt all alone. I had never been anywhere by myself. The bus was scheduled to arrive within the hour. I decided to take a short stroll down the street. I heard a loud noise coming from a bar. As I walked in front of the bar, a crowd came outside, and then there was a fight. I turned around and went back to the bus station.

The bus arrived and on schedule. I was really surprised to see that I did not have to sit in the back or behind a line on the floor. So, for the very first time in my life, I sat in the front seat.

I arrived in Detroit and took a taxi to my uncle and

aunt's house on the East side. I felt somewhat guilty staying with them because they had two boys and my uncle was on disability. L. H., as he was called, was good-looking and could really sing. My aunt's name was Alice. She was my favorite relative.

I wanted to take care of my aunt and uncle, but I could not find a job. Since I was not a native of Detroit, I was placed on non-residential status whenever I took a government examination. I did not know it at the time, but my Dad was sending them money to take care of me.

I got the surprise of my life when my dad and a neighbor from Fort Pierce came to the house about a month later. As usual, he was not very cordial towards me. He had made arrangements with another relative of ours in Detroit to buy a GMC truck-tractor. They stayed a couple days and drove the rig back to Fort Pierce. He had purchased three flatbed trailers already down home. His plan was to haul citrus fruit from the groves directly to the various juice plants. He also had a contract with a firm to transport fertilizer to different areas of Florida.

When I was not job hunting, I spent most of the time with my uncle at home. The gang activity in the neighborhood frightened me. Someone was always getting shot or killed nearby.

A neighbor of my relatives suggested that I try to get an audition at Motown (formerly Hitsville, USA). I asked around and learned that it was very difficult to get auditioned there. The agency was located on the Grand Boulevard in Detroit. Famous performers such as The Supremes, Temptations, and Stevie Wonder were headquartered there.

It took a few months, but I finally got auditioned by Brian Holland. Among his hits was "Please Mr. Postman" for The Marvelettes. He thought that I had a good singing voice.

He asked that I return to the studio in a month's time, as they had to go on tour.

I had auditions at other agencies. All of them had accepted me and wanted to put me to work right away. I had my eyes only on becoming a performer with Motown.

I called my parents in Florida. I told them that there was a possibility I would become a professional singer. Not surprisingly, my dad was not overwhelmed. He asked, "How old are you?"

I told him, "Twenty."

"Have you registered for the draft yet?"

I told him that I forgot.

He said, "The FBI has been by my office twice, looking for you." He suggested that I come home, as soon as possible and contact the people at the local draft board.

I figured I could get this resolved and then return to Motown. I went by Greyhound bus to Florida. It was fun sitting in the front seat behind the driver.

When I arrived home, I contacted at the draft board and they scheduled a hearing for me. I was a bit nervous about this hearing, but I was hoping that everything could be resolved and I could return to Detroit and to Motown to live my dream.

I had to go to the federal court in Fort Pierce. The Magistrate was a white woman named Louise Miller. She asked me, "Why haven't you registered for the service?"

I replied, "I was not trying to dodge the draft. I just forgot to register."

She asked, "Where have you been these last few months?"

I told her that I was trying to become a musician in Detroit. She told me that I would be making plenty of music where she was going to send me. I asked her the whereabouts of this place. She said, "To the federal penitentiary, in Atlanta, Georgia."

I could hardly hold back the tears in my eyes.

She added, "You will be making music with a sledgehammer busting rocks at the prison."

She told me to sit down, and said that she would get back to me. She said she needed to think about what she was going to do with me. After she had heard a few other cases, she called me back and said, "I've decided what to do with you. Instead of prison, I'm sending you to the military. Expect to be in the army within three months." I was sad, because I would not have a singing career, but glad, of course, because I would not have to go to prison.

# *In the Army*

In March 1964, I along with others, was on the way to the induction center in Miami, Florida. I was wondering whether I would ever return to Motown after I was discharged. I surely wanted another audition and I was feeling determined to become a famous singer someday. I was wishing something would happen to the bus so we could return home. Then, as we were riding through the Palm Beach area, smoke started coming from beneath the bus. The driver pulled over in a turnout and we all exited. The brakes had been burned out. Another bus was dispatched to our location, and we were transported on to Miami. Well, I got half of it, something happened to the bus, but I was still headed for the induction center.

Later that evening, we black inductees were taken to a below average hotel located in a rough part of Miami. Whites were lodged in nice hotels in downtown. The next day, all inductees, black and white, had physicals, and were lectured to and sworn in together. I could not believe it – blacks and whites were actually doing things together.

The following day all of us boarded railroad cars en route to Fort Jackson, South Carolina. I was still astounded because I had never really interacted much with white people, other than those with whom or for whom I had worked. It was never tolerated where I grew up. In fact it was considered dangerous to associate with whites, but here we were playing cards, laughing, and joking together. There were a few whites who would not associate with us; they thought it wasn't the right thing to do. A few said that their parents would not approve of them mingling with blacks.

I was constantly looking around in the railroad car at the inductees. I could not believe we were in the same railroad car, since blacks always rode in separate cars from whites. I mean, segregation was still the way of life in the South. The Civil Rights Act wouldn't become law until the following year.

The next night we arrived in Columbia, South Carolina. NCO's were waiting for us in military buses at the station. They were shouting, and herding us into the buses. I had never heard anyone shouting like that except for my father. I did not think that I would last very long as I was very short-fused. Plus, it was very cold and we were only wearing our lightweight civilian clothing.

A few minutes later we were allowed to use the latrine (bathrooms). I had never heard the word latrine in my life. There must have been thirty to forty toilets in a row with no partitions. One could not poop in private any longer. I was amazed yet again because blacks and whites were all sitting on these commodes side by side. I flushed while sitting and jumped up screaming. I looked at a sign behind me stating not to flush while sitting, as the water in the bowl was hot. I had never heard of such a thing before.

The next day we were lined up for haircuts. I had already gotten a haircut before I left home. Each of us had been given $20.00 – the Army called it our "flying twenty" but I don't know why – so we could pay for our haircuts and some other things we needed. I told the NCO that I did not need a haircut. He said, "Get your ass in that line and shut up!" I really felt sorry for the guys with the long hair, who were placed at the head of the lines. They were really ridiculed by the NCO's and others. When their hair was cut, there were loud cheers.

*From Colored Town to Pebble Beach*

The first week in the army was called "Zero Week" and we were all still in civilian clothes. This one day we were in formation and a white NCO with a very heavy southern accent looked at me and said, "Leroy Jones, step forward." I didn't move. He looked upset. He glared at me and yelled, "Leroy Jones, god dammit, I told you to step forward." When I did not respond, he got right into my face and screamed, "Leroy Jones" at me again. I said, "I'm not Leroy Jones." The white soldier standing next to me told the NCO that he was Leroy Jones. The NCO looked embarrassed but didn't apologize for his mistake.

We were issued duffel bags and ordered to form a line in the building where various military articles were being issued. We were to walk down the line with the duffel bags opened and the civilian staff would toss the articles inside. I was dragging my bag on the floor just to annoy the personnel there. A black staffer asked me not to drag the bag. I continued to drag it anyway. He yelled at me. I told him if he yelled at me again I would kick the shit out of him. I continued to drag it. He yelled at me again. I jumped over the counter and reached for him. My intentions were to whip his ass. Instead I was apprehended and taken to the first sergeant where I was reprimanded. I was almost sent to the stockade. I was given a broom and ordered to sweep the base's laundry building. Yes, I had an attitude problem.

After spending a week in Fort Jackson, we were again transported by military buses to Fort Gordon, Georgia. We arrived one cold night. Again, NCO's were managing us like cattle. We were wearing our brand new fatigue uniforms, caps, and boots, and carrying our duffel bags.

Some of us were assigned to "C" Company where a guy named Mejia, a Puerto Rican, was our platoon sergeant. He was tough. We could not walk in the company; we had to run. Otherwise he would have us do a whole lot of push-ups.

I was platoon guide. A white soldier did not like the idea of a nigger soldier giving him orders. He told me that he was going to kick my ass. One weekend, he had his chance. We wrestled outside of the barracks, and I kicked the shit out of him. We were friends from then on.

While in basic training I learned to buff floors, whitewash walls, make a tight bunk, and cook. Yes, that was basic training, all right. A cook was needed to assist the mess sergeant. I told them I had been a prep cook at the Waldorf Astoria. Of course that wasn't true. I had never cooked professionally in my life. Nor had I ever been near the Waldorf Astoria.

We got our first pass off the base. A Mexican, a white, and me went into nearby Augusta with the intention of eating a nice lunch, in a nice restaurant. I noticed mostly white soldiers were downtown and just a handful of blacks. I could not understand this until we walked into this restaurant and were met by the owner, who said to us, "The white boy can come in here, but we don't allow spicks and niggers in here." We just turned around, left the restaurant, and returned to the post.

So outside of the post life was still segregated. Black soldiers patronized black businesses only. I chose to stay on the post until I would be transferred to some other base outside of the South.

After basic training, I was chosen to go to Leadership School, also at Fort Gordon, where I had some infantry training and was learning to be a leader.

It was there I met a young country boy, with the surname Hughes. He was from the hills of Virginia and had never seen a black person before. He was in my platoon. Most of the guys made fun of him because he was like the television character, Gomer Pyle, but I got along with him just fine. Hughes was like my shadow; always following me around. He said, "I like you, DuVal, because you don't make fun of me. You treat me like I'm a human being." I could not believe I would ever hear that from a white guy; him appreciating having me for a friend.

Hughes was in my room listening to the radio when we heard that my favorite race car driver, Fireball Roberts, had been killed. That was a sad time for me. A few days later it got worse. Hughes came into my room, yelling, "DuVal, please don't let them take me away!" I did not understand what he was talking about. A few moments later, a warrant officer and two NCO's came to get him. The officer said that Hughes is going to be discharged, because he had lied about his age to get into the service. He was only seventeen years old. I was dumbfounded. As they were taking him, he was pleading with me not to let them take him. I stood there helpless. There was nothing I could do. I can still see him, in the back of that military sedan, looking back at me pleadingly. Oftentimes I wonder his whereabouts. I wish I could have kept in touch with him.

After Leadership School I went to the Military Police School, also at Fort Gordon. I had no intentions of becoming an MP. I wanted to become a diesel mechanic. But it seemed my military career was planned by someone other than me, and I had no idea who. Maybe it was just the system. Anyway, I volunteered for a third year.

My buddy, Errol Hunter, and I were still together from day one in the service. I was once again a platoon guide and so was he.

Over the years I realized that racial prejudice will always exist. In my platoon I had a different kind of prejudice. My platoon was composed of Mormons upstairs and rednecks downstairs. There was always an argument of some sort between the two. Mormons would have their religious discussions and the rednecks were of the mind that if someone was not a southern Baptist, he was nobody. I had to resolve countless confrontations. I made friends with a number of whites while in the service. Growing up, I'd never thought that would ever happen in my lifetime.

Something happened that, looking back was funny, but sure wasn't at the time. The company went into the forest to learn map reading and how to use a compass. My buddy Errol and I were with a bunch of city boys who were afraid of spiders, insects, and snakes. We were tired of hearing their complaints, so we thought up a little scheme. We handed them our map and compass and told them that we had to pee and we'd catch up with them in a few moments. Instead we ran into the thick forest and out of their sight. Our intention was to let them find their way back to the base camp by themselves. We were laughing so hard we had to sit on a log to gather our wits about us. We were imagining them being frightened to death.

It turned out the joke was on us. We were lost instead. It was almost midnight when we finally returned to the base camp. The city boys had already found base camp with no problem. By the time we found camp, those guys had already eaten and gone to sleep. We were the laughing stock of the company for a while.

A few weeks later, we graduated MP school and were assigned to Bremerhaven, Germany. We went to the library to read about that area. I could not wait to get there because I wanted to see a real Oktoberfest.

Much to our surprise, though maybe we shouldn't have been surprised since this was the Army, our orders were changed. We were headed south to bolster the troops in the Panama Canal Zone who were having problems with Pan Nationals there. They had burned buildings and were threatening to take over the Zone. So we went back to the library and read about Panama.

A large number of soldiers boarded the ship. We were all assigned to the Panama Canal Zone (USAR Command). We were told that we would be at sea for seven days. The only stop would be in Puerto Rico, to pick up troops who were also assigned to Panama. We would have to pull guard duty 24/7.

As we were sailing from the Army terminal, I heard a loud scream. It came from a 250-pound black soldier. A few of us tried to comfort him. He said that he was a country boy and had never been away from home before. He was homesick and wanted to go home. He had never sailed nor even seen the ocean before. It took a few minutes to calm him down.

The enlisted men were on the bottom deck of the ship; the officers and their families were on the top. Each morning we had to get into formation for the muster (roll call). There was a problem with me. I had to report to the Sergeant Major every morning because I was supposedly AWOL. It was some paperwork mistake. I asked, "How can I be AWOL while at sea? Where else would I be but on the ship.?" He said that I would be put in the brig if I'm AWOL again. I told him that every morning I would be in the front row when my name is called. Every day at muster I made it a point to be accounted for.

A couple of days later our ship docked in Cristobal, Panama. There we boarded a train that could get from the Atlantic to the Pacific in one hour. It's only sixty miles away.

As I said, in the library at Fort Gordon, some of us read about Panama. It has jungles, swamps, snakes, and alligators. We saw the jungle and swamps from the train, and we were kind of disappointed because that was where we thought we were going to be assigned.

But before long, we arrived in Balboa. We were less

disappointed when we saw a bunch of beautiful women at the depot. Military buses were waiting for us MP's there. We were transported to Fort Clayton.

Our barracks were just a short distance from the Panama Canal. We could actually see activity at the locks from our windows. There were no glass panes in the windows just screens to keep the insects out. It was never cold because this area was just north of the Equator. The barracks had extended eaves to keep the rain from coming into the building.

I was assigned to a platoon billeted on the second floor of the three-story barracks. My bunk was between two white soldiers, and both guys were really nice. I made friends with other black soldiers, especially NCO's. It was really nice to see black platoon leaders. The entire company was diverse. To me, this was really something. I was still struggling, trying to get used to integration, and I wondered why it was taking me so long, except that I knew things were different here, but they were still the same in the Deep South, which I called home. I could still recall what an old black woman in Fort Pierce said to me, "Because a white man smiles at you, doesn't mean he likes you." I always kept that in my mind.

Across the street from our barracks was a bowling alley. Since blacks could not bowl in my hometown, I had never learned and I decided now was the time to change that. There was no automation in those days. San Blas Indians retrieved the balls and set the pins. The PX was nearby as well. Employees there were mostly descendants of the blacks who had built the canal, during the early 1900's.

Our company manned military gates and patrolled on the Pacific side of the isthmus. We MP's wore starched khaki uniforms, white and black service caps, black patent leather gear with a .45 caliber automatic pistol on our hip, and tall, black, shiny boots. I had a thirty-inch waistline in those days.

## From Colored Town to Pebble Beach

Curundu was where the civilian Panama Canal employees lived. It was on the border between the Canal Zone and the Republic of Panama. Impoverished Panamanians lived just outside of the Curundu gate. They were housed in old shanties made of tin and strips of wood, which were constructed over a dirty and stagnant pond. They ate bananas from nearby trees, and out of garbage cans. Some of the women there worked as maids in the Canal Zone.

Panama was a very interesting place. I had a friend, James Brown – no, not the famous singer, but yes, he was black – and he and I patronized the finest of businesses in Panama City. Two were the Panama Hilton, where there was an organist who played nightly, and the El Continental. Both had gambling casinos.

It was in Balboa where I heard my first classical music concert. A symphony orchestra from Chile played Beethoven's Violin Concerto in D. I was elated with the sounds. I'd never heard such fine music live and in person. Also, I liked the fact that the audience was diverse and not segregated.

The very first time I ate Chinese food was in Panama City. It was so good; I patronized the Chinese restaurant once or twice a week. In the Deep South, Asians had restaurants in White Town, but we blacks could not patronize them because of segregation.

Our company tailor was an elderly black Panamanian we called Pops. He was probably in his eighties. His shop was on the bottom floor of the barracks. He used to tell me stories about the building of the Canal. He said that his father worked on the canal at the turn of the century. He said that the white workers were provided housing during that time. The blacks lived in tents, they had no days off, they had fewer privileges, and most of them died from malaria.

The blacks, he said, were always the last to get medical attention, which was why so many of them died. When I had been in Panama only a few days, I went to town on a pass. I saw a black guy standing on the corner. I asked him a question. He replied, "No comprendo."

So I got to like Panama quickly. Here's another reason why. Whenever I took a shower, I would sing aloud in Spanish. Of course, with no window panes, so I could be heard outside in the streets. Very often there would be some Panamanian ladies outside listening and applauding.

# <u>*My Panama Tour*</u>

After spending time manning gates, I was in a car patrolling the officer's residential area. It was shortly after noon time when, as I was passing one of the homes, I saw something in one of the windows that was so unusual, I backed up, parked, got out of the car for a better look. Sure enough, I saw someone's butt in the window. It was a burglar who had gotten stuck. I pulled him out and to the ground where he struggled with me for a bit before I subdued him. He had a replica of a .45 caliber pistol in his belt, which I relieved him of, and then I handcuffed him, and placed him in my patrol car. It turned out that he was a Pan National who had been committing burglaries on all the bases. I turned him over to the Canal Zone Police.

One time, while patrolling the Curundu area, I was dispatched to an apartment fire. I arrived just a minute or two before the fire personnel. Heavy smoke was coming from the windows. I knew the man who lived there; he was a heavy drinker. I kicked the door open and entered the dwelling. He was on the couch passed out. With the help of one of the firemen, I got him outside. He had been cooking a pot of beans and had laid down and fallen asleep. It was the pot of beans that had burned, causing the heavy smoke. Fortunately, the apartment did not burn.

There was a call I responded to from a sergeant who said that there was a boa constrictor in his washer machine.

I went to his barracks and saw the snake coiled inside. It was then that I noticed that the sergeant was wearing a jungle emblem on his fatigue uniform shirt. I asked him if he had gone to the Jungle Warfare School in Fort Gulick. He said that he had been an instructor there for a while. He went on to say that he ate monkeys, snakes, and alligators and anything else to survive. I turned around and got into my patrol car. He demanded to know what I was going to do about the snake. I told him that since he had eaten snakes before, he had his dinner and enough for tomorrow's lunch right there in that washer machine. And then I drove off.

Screams were heard by neighbors in this NCO residential area. When I arrived, neighbors were pointing to the residence where the screams were heard. I went inside, thinking I was going to see an injured woman. Instead, there was a sergeant protecting his face with his arms and hands, and his Japanese wife was standing in front of him in a karate stance. He was the one who was screaming, as she was chasing him around the house, slapping and kicking him. She explained to me later that she was just tired of him yelling at her all of the time. They had been married twenty years.

Rio Hatta was a base camp, located many miles north of the Canal Zone on the beach. I was assigned there with the 4th Mechanized Infantry. Our maneuvers there were conducted with heavy artillery, both on the ocean and in the jungle. Along with a Guardia Nacional policeman, I kept the peace in the surrounding towns which were off limits to the military. There were prostitutes who had all types of venereal diseases. One soldier sneaked out one night, became engaged with a prostitute and caught a venereal disease that was so bad, he had to be flown to Walter Reed

Hospital in Washington, D. C.

One night around midnight, I heard faint conversations coming from the area of our mess hall. I walked over and saw little children with bags made of hemp, getting the scraps out of the garbage cans. I had never seen anything like this in my life. I approached them and some of them ran. Those who remained told me that they were taking food home to their families.

A short time later, I met some of the villagers. Most lived in mud huts and had large families. I could not believe what I had seen. Others lived in old wooden shacks. Even though it was tough for me in segregated America, I really felt better about being an American – even a black American living in the South – after seeing the conditions in which these people lived.

I accompanied the infantry many times to Rio Hatta and had lots of experiences. That is another book.

The USO provided our troops with entertainment. We asked them to tell us about what was happening in the world (United States). They said that the Beatles were high on the pop charts. We were told that they were English and had funny hairstyles.

I became an Accident Investigator. My duty was, obviously, to investigate accidents involving military personnel and their dependents anywhere in the Canal Zone. One rainy day I was investigating a two-car accident. Three other drivers were trying to see what was going on and ran into both cars that were already involved. Fortunately, no one was hurt. I was there for hours.

I used to suck on lollipops and kept a box of them in the patrol car with me. I was investigating an accident in a residential area, and was interviewing a woman there. I had my hand behind my back holding a candy. I didn't want her to see me sucking on it because it might have seemed unprofessional. But when it seemed that I was going to be at that scene for a while, I decided to take a big bite out of that candy and suck on it as I investigated the accident. I brought the lollipop out from behind my back, and without looking at it, I put it in my mouth. The problem was that a great big stink bug had gotten stuck on it while I was holding it behind my back, and I had bitten into it. I was so disgusted, I immediately began throwing up. People who gathered at the scene of the accident thought it was very funny and they were all laughing.

I used to reprimand a certain civilian working for the military for speeding all of the time. I told him the way he drove he would probably kill himself or someone else before too long. One day, he was driving his '63 Ford over the Thatcher-Ferry bridge. He was speeding and drove underneath a truck-tractor rig, and got decapitated. It was a sad day.

Accident investigators slept in the office at the MP Headquarters when we had 24-hour duty. I used to read about the racial demonstrations and other ordeals that were making headlines in the United States. I wondered sometimes what I was doing down there in the Canal Zone when I could be fighting for an end to segregation back in my own country.

A white soldier told me that where he was from, a black man had saved a white boy from drowning in a lake. His mother was glad her son was saved, but she was angry because it had to be a black man that saved him. She took the boy home and scrubbed him good.

I was reading about the black Olympian Jesse Owens. He had humiliated Adolf Hitler's athletes and his Nazi myth about "Aryan supremacy" back in 1936 by winning four gold medals. When he returned to the United States, he was given a ticker-tape parade, but afterwards he was treated like a second-class citizen. He could not stay in some hotels and could not eat in most restaurants.

After the Second World War, few black veterans could find decent jobs, and also had come back to living under segregation. I also read about the black soldiers who were guarding German POW's in The States in Georgia, but they could not eat in the restaurants there. The POWs could, but not their black guards. The guards had to watch the POWs' eat from the outside. This was a shame. Of course, the Armed Forces were integrated at the time I was in, and I got to thinking that when I returned to the states, would I be living in that segregated world again?

Hattie McDaniel, who won an Oscar for playing Mammy in "Gone with the Wind," had to come through a back door and sit at a table alone at the ceremony. This was a shame as well.

I must say that relative to living in the South, duty in Panama was very good. At first, I was supposed to have been discharged there. I decided that I wanted to stay and become a Canal Zone Policeman. I had been working hand-in-hand with the CZ police the entire time I was there and I liked the people and the operation there.

In May, 1966, my buddy, Errol Hunter, and I were informed that we would be transferred to Fort Ord in California for our remaining seven months of service. In July, I was sent back to the States for a month's leave at home before being shipped out to California. I had mixed feelings about going back. I really enjoyed not having to deal with segregation in the Zone, and didn't like the idea of having to face it in the South. Every place in the Zone was integrated, even the schools. I really didn't want to return to the States because in most places blacks were still demonstrating for equal rights. Some of those biggest demonstrations in 1965 had been led by Dr. Martin Luther King, Jr. They were mainly protesting discrimination in black voter registration. During that year, the Senate had passed the Voting Rights Act. This guaranteed all people the right to vote without fear of intimidation, reprisal, or arbitrary barriers.

The day I was supposed to leave for the States, I was given an escort to the airport by a number of my fellow MP's. What a sendoff! What really blew me away was that most of the MP's were white. I teared up. There was also a number of patrol cars on the tarmac.

This was my first flight on a commercial airplane. As the plane took off, I watched the MP cars disappear below, knowing I would probably never see any of those men again. I was teary-eyed for much of the flight.. We were headed to Charleston, South Carolina. After arriving at Charleston, I boarded a Greyhound bus for home.

While riding the bus, I had to remember that I was once again in the Deep South. I remembered Medgar Evers, a civil rights worker, who was shot and killed in front of his house in 1963. At the time the case was still unsolved. Despite the Civil Rights Act of 1964 and the Voting Rights Act of 1965, segregation was still happening. It brought back great memories of being in Panama. I thought of a film festival that was held in the Zone where Troy Donahue was the featured guest and I was his escort. That was so much fun.

And how I served on both General O'Meara's and General Alger's cordons, taking care of their security. I met many foreign generals and heads of states. I remember one night a celebrity was performing at the officers club at Fort Amador. We were told that General Alger would attend. I was assigned to the road on which his chauffeured military vehicle was to come. My orders were to make certain that no other vehicles interfered with his arrival. Suddenly someone drove an old Chrysler up to where I was standing. I stopped it. I said, "Please move on. I'm expecting the general to arrive any second now." There was laughter inside of the vehicle. I asked, "What's so funny?" and stooped down to speak with the driver. I found that I was looking right in the general's face. I locked my heels tight as I sprang to attention. (You could not have pried my feet apart with a crowbar.) The general said, "At ease, Pat. I decided to give my driver a break tonight." He and his wife left laughing. I had almost died of surprise. That wasn't the way things were in Florida.

The bus made a stop in Vero Beach just ten miles from my hometown, Fort Pierce. I remembered when I was a little boy that the Brooklyn Dodgers did their spring training there. The black members of that team also had some problems with segregation down there.

Nothing had really changed. Segregation was still the ongoing thing. My mind was made up. I decided to return to Panama after I was discharged from the army. I wanted – I needed – to get away from the racial oppression.

When I came home, none of my family recognized me. My mom thought that I was a burglar and called my dad, who was still a deputy sheriff. He was patrolling nearby and came home. He recognized me. We all laughed about the weight I had gained while I was in Panama.

Still, there were some good things about coming home, like seeing old friends. I had a policeman friend, Bill Ellis, from childhood. He was always around when I was in trouble. I had been a wannabe thug when I was growing up. He told me that I needed to shape up, otherwise someone was going to kill me. I was looking forward to seeing Bill, so he could see that I had shaped up.

My dad allowed me to use his detective car to visit some friends. I saw Bill with Jiggs Minus patrolling together. I stopped them to let them know I'd be home for almost a month. Bill asked that I stay put for a few moments as they had a domestic call to answer around the corner.

A few moments later, I heard gunshots and screaming. A woman ran towards us saying the policemen were shot. I saw a deputy sheriff driving code-three in that direction. Suddenly, others came from that area stating that Bill and Jiggs had both been shot.

I got into my Dad's car and spoke with his dispatcher. I asked that she tell my dad what had occurred and I'd be home to pick him up. Within five minutes, I turned the corner and saw Dad standing at the edge of our driveway waiting for me. He drove back to the scene code-three, after he dropped me off nearby.

Sadly, Bill died at the scene. Jiggs had a gunshot wound to his stomach but survived. Bill had one hell of a funeral. There were police officers from all over the south. White and black, hundreds of motorized policemen. A pall hung my entire leave, as Bill had been my hero since I was a boy.

I spent the rest of the month visiting with old friends, and before long, I was on my way to Fort Ord.

Because the airlines were on strike at the time, I boarded an Express Greyhound bus to San Francisco. This was a four-day trip, and another black soldier, who was reassigned to the Presidio in San Francisco, and I were seated together. The Post House restaurants in the South were still segregated, but things got a little better as we traveled west.

The bus stopped in Salinas, California, which is where I got off to change to a bus that would take me to Fort Ord. I wished my partner Godspeed for his new assignment in San Francisco.

On the way to Fort Ord, I passed beautiful farmlands and fields. John Steinbeck's writings had been required reading in our high school, and I could not get over being where Steinbeck lived. I could not wait to actually see Cannery Row and Doc Ricketts' Lab. As the bus arrived in Fort Ord, I saw a lamb for the first time in my life. He was enclosed in a small pen. Little kids were petting it.

My barracks were adjacent to the bus station. I got off and reported to the first sergeant, at the 54th MP Co. He had been expecting me and he called my buddy, Errol Hunter, who had arrived three weeks prior. He said that Errol was assigned to the stockade, instead of patrol, because of a personnel shortage.

I was supposed to have been an accident investigator but I was also to be assigned to the stockade. I told him I had no confinement experience. He replied that I would learn. He was right. I did learn.

I enjoyed working in the stockade. I worked the swing shift. There were quite a number of troops housed there for many different reasons. Some had gone AWOL, some were felons, deserters, and on the other end of the scale, conscientious objectors. There was a chapel inside the facility. On Sundays, a chaplain would conduct religious services there.

Gays were housed in a separate section of the stockade for their own good. Most inmates detested gays and would do bodily harm, even kill them, if they could. I had never associated with a gay person before, and I learned a lot from them.

I made friends with James Lancaster and his family. His

wife worked at a nearby snack bar. They lived in Seaside, a town that adjoins Fort Ord. James had retired from the Army. He worked as a custodian in the school system and umpired baseball games. I spent a lot of time with him and his son, Jimmy, going to sporting events and movies.

Seaside was a racially diverse community. The schools were integrated. Blacks could buy gas with no problems, eat in restaurants, and engage in the many other normal activities that blacks could not do in the Deep South. I saw blacks working in banks, chain stores, and everywhere else. Again, this surprised me. I had never seen anything like it before. I had never even tried to eat in a real restaurant or a coffee shop outside of the South because I thought that I would not get served. I still had the South mentality in me.

I did walk around Cannery Row. In those days, the old canneries were always working. They would soon become converted to new businesses.

I used to go to Pacific Grove, another peninsula city, and sit by the ocean reading my Sherlock Holmes books.

Another buddy of mine, George Whyte, who had also been stationed in Panama and had been discharged from Fort Ord, was working at the Bank of America in Seaside. We met one day to talk about old times. He told me that he was a member of Hayes Chapel, a Methodist church located in Seaside. He invited me to come with him to sing an Easter Cantata there. I agreed, but warned him that I had not sung in a church since I was a child. As it turned out, not only did I sing in the cantata, but I joined the church's choir as well. And shortly afterwards, I started singing solos. Major Samuel Brown and Mrs. Elizabeth Wells accompanied me on the piano and organ. I quickly became a well-known songster, singing in different churches, at weddings, and various other events.

There were times when I, along with other MP's, would transport prisoners to Fort Leavenworth, Kansas. We would get bussed to the Oakland Army Terminal, then over to the train station. There, the army had sleeper cars for us to make the two-day trip to Lawrence, Kansas. We would guard our prisoners 24/7. Once we arrived in Lawrence, busses would transport us to the federal prison. There were also times when we flew to Kansas.

In January, 1967, I decided to return to Panama to check on my eligibility for the Canal Zone Police. Plus I wanted see my old friends there. I hopped a military transport at Travis Air Force Base which took me to McGuire Air Force Base in New Jersey. From there I flew to Miami and then to Tucuman Airport in Panama on Pan-Am I was so happy to be back.

I went to the CZP station in Balboa. I was still third on the list for a position with the Canal Zone Police. I had planned to either return to Panama or return to Florida A&M as a student. I had only a couple of months to make up my mind. After visiting with most of my old friends, I decided I would rather return to Panama than go back to Florida and live with the racism

A week later, I returned to Fort Ord, and I learned from James Lancaster that his brother-in-law, Willard Stallworth, wanted to speak with me. Stallworth asked me directly what were my plans after I was discharged from the Army. I told him about my intention to return to join the Canal Zone Police. He said to me,"Tomorrow, you and I are going to Salinas to see the Sheriff. He is a friend of mine." I told him that I'd go with him, but that my mind was really set on returning to Panama.

The next day, we met with the Sheriff in his office in Salinas. He told me that he needed new deputies, and that blacks never applied for some unknown reason. He didn't want anyone thinking he was a bigot. He urged me to take the exam coming up in July which was three months away. I told him that I would give it some thought.

In March of 1967, I was discharged from the army. I decided to stay with the Lancasters until exam time in July. Shortly after my discharge, I took the exam for work at the Bank of America. When I finished the exam, I felt good about having passed. In fact, except for a question about square roots, it had seemed very easy to me. So I was dumbfounded when I received a letter from them saying that I failed the test.

Two weeks later, the secretary I knew who was leaving that office told me that I passed the exam. The only problem I missed, he told me, was the square root problem. The fact was, he said, the administrator did not want to hire too many blacks. I was really convinced that racism existed all over; not just in the Deep South. I did not bother to contact that administrator.

Blacks were still demonstrating in the Deep South, and in fact in many parts of the country, but I was not disposed to returning to Florida to live.

In July of 1967, a friend of mine, Willie Williams, drove me to the Salinas High School, where the sheriff's examination was being administered. I had no idea the whereabouts of this school as I had only been to Salinas once. I was late but asked to take the exam anyway.

Afterwards, I left a self-addressed special delivery envelope with the people who administered the exam. I asked if they could inform me of whether I had passed the exam or not. The next day I left for Florida by Greyhound bus to see my folks and my friends.

It was a four day trip by bus. All I did the whole way was think about how life would be when I returned home. I was tired of whites calling me names and not allowing blacks to enjoy a normal life and do everyday things. But I was torn between living again in Panama and becoming a student at FAMU where I had been accepted. And of course I was wondering whether I had passed deputy exam.

As I traveled east on the bus, matters became somewhat worse. Blacks still could not sit and eat in Post House restaurants.

The trip was very tiresome. The bus was full; the only vacant seat was next to me. I was the only black passenger. I don't think any white person wanted to sit next to me. We stopped in Biloxi, Mississippi, for a break. I did not bother to get off as I thought I would get into trouble just trying to use the restroom or purchasing a snack. I remained in my seat. A few moments later, it was time to move on. A white middle-aged woman wanted to board the bus, but she said she would wait for the next one, as she did not want to sit next to a nigger. I felt so bad, I wanted to cry. I heard snickering and laughter coming from the white passengers. I was so embarrassed. I said to myself, "Welcome to the old South."

A day and a half later on Saturday afternoon, I arrived at my parents' house in Fort Pierce. Of course, they were glad to see me. We were all sitting on the front porch, talking about old times, and my dad said, "By the way, Son, I received this letter in the mail. I thought it was for me, until I opened it."(My Dad is Patrick, Sr. and I'm Junior.)

It was the letter concerning the deputy's exam. I read it aloud to my parents. It stated that I had passed the written exam and asked if I could I come to the sheriff's office that coming Tuesday afternoon to appear before an oral board.

My mom said, "Now boy, you be careful. If it doesn't work out, you just come back home." And my dad, he was proud. There were stories in the newspapers in Fort Pierce and Miami showing him, he was a sergeant then, holding up a picture from 1952 when he was made one of the first black deputies in the South. The headline was something like "Lawman is surprised that his son is a lawman, too."

Not long after that surprise, I drove around my hometown and saw that little had changed. The schools were still segregated, along with everything else. My decision was made. I went to a travel agency, bought an airline ticket for Monterey, and left the Monday morning before I was due back there to appear for the orals to become a deputy. I had not even unpacked my suitcase.

I gave some money to my mom and had only a hundred dollars to my name. I was very nervous, because even if I passed the orals, I knew I could be put on a waiting list. Then what? I prayed hard on that flight back to Monterey.

My friends, Robert and Delores Bates, allowed me to sleep on their couch at Fort Ord. On that momentous Tuesday afternoon, I went before the orals board. After the interview, I was told that I would be informed of the results in a few days; that my background had to be checked. The board was all white. I did not think I had a chance.

Monday morning of the following week, the Under-sheriff, Jimmy Rodriguez, called me on the telephone and said, "Congratulations, you're one of us now." He told me that I was now a full-fledged deputy sheriff and I needed to be sworn in that very morning. He asked if I had a car. I told him not yet. He said that he would pick me up himself within the hour. I gave him directions to find the Bates' residence.

Not much later he picked me up and on the way to the swearing in he started explaining the job to me. He said, "And by the way, you're the first black deputy this county has ever had." I was shocked to learn that, and thought about my dad being the first black deputy sheriff in Saint Lucie County.

The undersheriff and I met with the sheriff in his office. The sheriff, Jack Davenport, congratulated me and welcomed me aboard. He said womanizing, being in debt, and alcoholism could cause me to lose this job. Those weren't big worries for me.

# *Deputy DuVal*

I was sworn in on August 30, 1967 at ten that morning in a room in the detective division in Salinas. Afterwards, I was told that I was needed immediately to develop information on a murder which had recently been committed in north Monterey County. I was being used because I wasn't known to anyone in the area. That afternoon, I was handcuffed by Sergeant Bud Cook – who later became sheriff – and was escorted to the county jail. There I was booked under a false name for a felony I was supposed to have committed in King City. Then I was put in a holding cell with a bunch of illegal aliens. (It's funny the things you remember, like the fact that there was only one toilet in the cell and it was being used every other minute.)

Afterwards, I was dressed in denim coveralls and placed in an isolated cell with two suspects related to the murder. I was in this cell to see if I could get additional evidence for the prosecution. They looked me over and asked what my beef was. I told them that I had ripped off a gas station down in King City. The cell was really small. My bunk was across from the toilet. I slept with my back against the wall. I spent most of the time shadow boxing and making unusual noises. I was never bothered. I wanted them to think that I was an animal. It worked.

We were served three meals daily by trustees and a deputy. The deputies had no idea who I was. To them I was just another prisoner. I would ask for extra food in Spanish and sometimes Portuguese because the deputy serving the food spoke the language and I'd picked up some of it when I was doing stockade duty at Fort Ord. That was maybe why most of the time I got the extra food. My cellmates thought I was an "all right" guy. I was incarcerated for more than a week. One of the suspects turned state's evidence and the prosecution got a conviction. I'd like to think I helped turning him but I can't say that I did.

I was released from the jail and given some time to purchase my uniforms up in San Jose. That was the closest uniform store in those days. I also needed a car, but hadn't established any credit. I spoke with my retired army buddy, George Whyte, who was now an employee at the Bank of America. (Yes, the bank where I had passed the application test but where they already had enough black employees so I "failed.") George directed me to Jerry Lucido, who was a reputable loan officer.

I was nervous as I did not think I would get a loan because I was new in the area and black. In the Deep South, if a black managed to get a loan, the interest rates would be astronomical. I explained to Jerry my dilemma and my concerns. Then somehow we started to talk about music. I told him that I was an opera singer. He was thrilled to hear that. Both of us broke into song right there in the bank. It was Italian opera, and we must have been good because a few minutes later, the patrons in the bank broke into applause.

Jerry told me to find the car I wanted and come back to him with the price, and he would give me the loan. I was dumbfounded. I never thought I would get a loan without references, and I didn't really have any references since I was new to the area and new to my job. I thanked George for recommending me to Jerry, and then I went looking for a car.

I went to the Volkswagen dealership in Seaside and saw a black car salesman. I stared at him for more than a minute without saying a word. He asked me why I was staring at him. I told him that I had never seen a black car salesman in my entire life. Where I came from in the Deep South, blacks worked as detailers or custodians, but never as salesmen. I apologized to him, and told him how embarrassed I felt.

I was going to buy a VW from that salesman, but instead I found a '59 Triumph for sale for $500 from a private party and I thought that would be a better deal for me. I went to the bank and Jerry agreed. And he gave me the loan.

I reported for work in Salinas, proudly wearing my new uniform. The first officer I rode with was Deputy Dick Swinscoe. He was a very nice guy. He always kept a smile on his face. I felt nervous for a while, but he helped me to feel at ease.

Being the first black deputy in Monterey County was tough. The news media from San Francisco and other areas wanted a story from me. I asked that they speak with the sheriff for information about me. He later told the news media that I passed the exam like everyone else, and I just happened to be black.

The undersheriff assigned me to the Monterey Substation. When I reported to the sub, I knew that I would not receive a warm welcome. I had learned that a meeting was held prior to my arrival, informing the deputies that a black deputy had been assigned to the sub. The deputies were asked who would like to work with him. No hands were raised.

I met the deputy who did my background check, Roger Chatterton. He never said so, but I believe he was criticized by other deputies for checking on me, finding me all right, and thereby getting me hired. Some of the other deputies thought that he should have come up with something that would prevent my appointment. Roger told me that he did not have a prejudiced bone in his body and had no problem doing my background check.

Boy, could Roger eat. I have seen him put away a half dozen eggs, most of a pound of bacon, four slices of toast, and other food at a single sitting. He got very few invites to other people's homes for dinner, but I had the occasion to eat at his home.

While shaking hands, and looking at the smiling faces of some deputies, I remembered again the adage from back home that a white man shaking hands with you and smiling doesn't mean he likes you. I knew no one wanted to work with me. Little did they know that wasn't going to stop me. There were a couple of deputies who told me that they didn't want to work with me. So what? I didn't particularly want to work with them either. But I sure didn't like feeling that this was like being in the segregated South again. Of course, not nearly as bad.

I had to wonder at times like this why I had taken this job. I guess I thought that I would be working in a part of the county that was mostly black. But in Monterey, most calls we dealt with were from whites. When I asked where was the black population in the county, someone said, "You're it." That was troublesome since I had never been to a white person's front door in my life. In the South, it would be justifiable homicide if a black was shot while standing at the door of a white. Even if a black was seen just walking in a white neighborhood at night, he could be shot.

After I had been in Monterey a short time, it was discovered that ammunition was being taken by someone without the approval of the station commander. Some people "naturally" thought it was me. I thought maybe someone was trying to frame me; that someone would find a way to get rid of me. I thought maybe I would not last very long on this job. But one day, all the deputies and staff were asked to come a darkened room. An infrared lamp was turned on. Nobody knew that infrared dust had been placed where the ammunition was kept. One of the deputies lit up like a Christmas tree. He was transferred to the jail.

In the South, there were numerous cases of police brutality involving blacks, and certainly very little justice. If the average black man was accused of committing a crime, most likely he would end up in state prison or on the chain gang. Hardly any of the cases had sufficient evidence. There was never an intense investigation.

When I started with the sheriff's office, there was a lot of pressure on me as I tried to cope with being part of integration. I knew the guys thought that I was a dummy and would never become a good deputy. So I studied my penal and civil codes religiously, but I guess I'd had to much of the segregation attitudes ingrained in me and it sometimes interfered with my studies.

One of my supervisors, Sergeant John Crisan, was originally from Romania. He was particularly nice and had a way of handling the public in a manner I could not believe. He had impeccable manners, even to a person who had committed a crime. I decided that if I lasted in this office, I was going to speak with the public in the same manner. I was surprised to have overheard other deputies complaining about his mannerisms. They thought the public should be dealt with more coldly. The truth was that John made them look bad.

I was really downright shocked when he asked me to join him and his family for dinner at his house, as I had never eaten at a white man's house before. But what a joyous time I had.

I had heard from outside sources that most deputies did

not like working with me. Some did not think it was fair that I worked where there were all whites. (I didn't either, but from a different perspective.) Some thought that it was not fair to have me answering complaints made by whites. Of course that lessened my confidence about keeping my job, and I was constantly watching my back. I didn't feel I had anywhere to turn to deal with this problem without sounding like I was whining. There were no human resources office in those days.

One of my instructors was an okay guy to partner with. He had just gone through a divorce and was quite upset about the situation. He had an apartment but could not cook. He had a refrigerator full of beer, TV dinners, Spam, and a dozen eggs that had green fungus on them. We called ourselves, the "I Spy" team as that was a popular television series at the time, starring Bill Cosby and Robert Culp.

One day while we were patrolling, he seemed to be sore about something. I asked him what was wrong. He said, "We're going to get some of my personal property back from my ex-wife." Soon we arrived at his former residence. He knocked at the door. His wife opened it and asked that we wait.

While we were standing there, he was looking through the door that was ajar. He said, "Look at that."

I asked, "Look at what?"

He said, "Her new boyfriend is reading a damned book lying on the couch that I worked so hard to make the money to buy."

She returned and said that she had decided to sell him his property and slammed the door in our faces. We left, without incident, but he was livid.

The deputies would stop at a popular coffee shop, Thom

Thumb's, which was located in the Del Monte Shopping Center. Whenever I was asked to go have coffee, I would say, "You guys go. I don't like coffee." It was a lie; I love coffee. I just did not think that I would be served. I know it sounds like I was slow catching on to how things were in California, at least where I was in Monterey, but I still had the South in me. Besides, I was not comfortable being with all that hostility in the Monterey sub-station. I wasn't wanted there.

Then one day after I'd been there for a while, one of the deputies said that some of the CHP (California Highway Patrol) officers wanted to meet me. A suggestion was made to meet at Thom Thumb's for a coffee break. I agreed to go. Usually, I would sit in the patrol car in the parking lot and listen for calls. But not this time.

Yes, I was nervous but I went and I met two CHP officers, Mac McCurdy and Leon Howard. We sat at the lunch counter, and the waitress, Shirley Smith, came over to give us some coffee. I did not think she would serve me. If you can believe it, I had never been in a white or mixed coffee shop before. She put a coffee cup in front of me, poured my coffee and said, "Hi, honey, would you like to have something to eat?" I almost fell off my stool. I could not believe I was served with no problems. Not only no problems, but she called me "Honey." I turned around to see if other patrons had heard her. At that moment, I forgot I was a deputy; I was looking for someone to protest. Happily, from then on, I drank coffee there and at Denny's. But that night I just had to call my parents in Florida to tell them about this. They still were not allowed to sit at lunch counters in those days.

Off duty, I always tried to mind my P's and Q's. I patronized piano bars and was never refused service. I would have a drink or two and then would leave for home.

I always felt someone was watching me and the number of drinks I was consuming.

An "old school" deputy told me that while most of the guys did not want to work with me, he would be more than happy to take me under his wing and work with me. What a great feeling that was. Yes, I knew that racial prejudice exists everywhere. I also knew that there were limits to how far I could go in this department. I was only hoping that when other blacks became deputies that my having been first would make it a little easier for them.

On several occasions, I applied to become a member of the rescue team. It was one of the sheriff department's duties to rescue lost hikers and motorists who had driven over the coastal cliffs. I was never selected. I felt like the kid who was never chosen to play on a team – some whites call it being like a red-headed step-child – but I almost never complained. But sometimes the pressure grew too much and I would tell the sheriff or the undersheriff that I was ready to resign, but they told me to just cool off. They said I had to think about how I would be thought of as a loser, and what it would mean for blacks who wanted to follow me into the department.

I saw the truth in what they were saying, and I also focused on the difference between where I'd been in the Deep South and the far more progressive Monterey County. Here on the Central Coast, there were black Greyhound bus drivers; there weren't any in the south. Nor were there white boundary lines on the floors of the buses here to separate white and black. Also, blacks could go to the drive-in theater in Salinas. Blacks were not allowed in drive-ins not anywhere in the South. I loved the drive-in and went as often as I could, taking a big bucket of Branding Iron chicken with me. In the South, when the circus came to town, there was always a colored entrance to the main tent. (As a small child, someone took me to a the Silas Green side show that was in White Town; blacks had to sit in the back. The characters had black skin and big white lips. I had never seen anything like that before and was very confused. I later learned that those characters were white and used makeup on their faces.) In Monterey, everyone used the same entrance.

It was around this time, the mid-to-late Sixties that I was watching the news every day on television. Oftentimes, on my breaks, I would go to the parking lot and sit in my car and listen to the news. (I know, listening to the news doesn't sound relaxing but I wanted to be informed of what was going on, and at the time, there was a lot of news about demonstrations being led by Dr. King in the Deep South. There were often casualties being reported.

Actually, there were demonstrations going on all over the country, in the North as well as the South. I felt guilty for not being there to fight for the cause of integration. In hindsight, I realize that I was fighting in my own way, and it was important, even though the segregation and the racism wasn't as severe or as blatant in Monterey County as it was in the Deep South.

I know I was slow in my thinking, but I finally realized that I was better off here than back home. I knew that it would be a disaster if I returned to the South. If life wasn't perfect here, at least it was better for me. I changed my mind about resigning.

I came across more and more evidence of the important difference between where I grew up and where I now lived. My instructor and I stopped at the Community Hospital of the Monterey Peninsula (CHOMP) which was on our beat.

It was one of the places where we would make our area checks frequently. While he was speaking with some of the staff in the emergency room, I was amazed to see – another first for me – white doctors treating blacks. I also saw black and white patients sharing rooms. I shook my head and smiled deep inside.

Many years ago in my hometown, blacks were not allowed to be patients in the hospital. My grandparents and other pioneer folk – they were some of the first blacks on the Atlantic Coast of Florida – got together, purchased a large house, bought hospital beds, and contracted a doctor to treat blacks. Later on, a large area in the basement of the local white hospital was converted into what was called the Colored Ward. Black and Seminole Indians were treated and became patients there. My mom worked there as an LPN. Whenever we called her at work, we would have to ask for the Colored Ward. Also, because white EMT's were not allowed to pick up blacks at accidents or for any other reason, black funeral directors would answer these calls.

The first black registered nurse I had ever seen was Aretha Ware at CHOMP. It was really something to see a black working hand-in-hand with whites. It was at the Community Hospital in Monterey. I was talking to a doctor who asked me who was my primary physician. I told him I only went to one doctor and his name was Dr. Benjamin Richards. He said that Richard was a surgeon. I didn't let on that I had no idea what a primary care doctor was. Down home, we had one doctor who took care of everything. Another good difference was that whenever I had to visit a doctor in Monterey, there was only one waiting room, not two.

One day at roll call, Lieutenant Henry Gilpin decided I should start patrolling alone. I would drive a '67 Plymouth patrol car. I was given a cheat card with the call signs. My call sign was "12-Monterey." He told me to learn the Carmel Valley area, take reports, and don't worry about a backup. Someone would be there to assist me, if I needed help. I was somewhere between excited and nervous to be going out like this on my own. But I did feel kind of special wearing our trademark Stetson hat which we had to keep on all of the time. One reason was so people would easily recognize us as deputies.

I was a little bit more concerned about the fact that the sheriff's office would soon start patrolling in Pebble Beach. This was a very affluent community, and very, very white. In fact, back then black people were not allowed to purchase property there.

I left the substation driving my own patrol car. I was aware that each time I would stop at a red light or a stop sign, I was being stared at. More than once someone would call the office and say that something seemed suspicious: they'd seen a black man driving a sheriff's cruiser and wearing a deputy's uniform. The callers thought maybe a white deputy had been kidnapped or killed by the black person driving the car.

During the first four to five hours, deputies patrolled alone. The remainder of the shift, they would patrol doubled up.

At approximately 8:00 the first night, I received my first call. The dispatcher called out on the radio, "12-Monterey."

I said to myself, "Oh Jesus! That's me she's calling." I was called again. I pulled into a turnout and answered. I was told to see a woman about a civil matter. Her neighbor's horse was coming into her yard and eating her flowers.

Even though it was a cold night, I was perspiring heavily. On the way to her house, I was having flashbacks. Never in the Deep South did one see a black man knocking at a white person's front door at night. I arrived moments later. I knocked on her front door. I could hear her walking towards the front door. Yes, I was nervous. I wouldn't have been surprised if she had started calling me names or slammed the door in my face.

When she opened the door, I introduced myself. I said, "Good evening, ma'am. I'm Deputy Pat DuVal."

She said, "Sure, come in."

What a wonderful surprise. My fears disappeared in a flash. She had acted normally asking me to come into her house. But, funny thing, for a moment I could not move I was so surprised. She asked, "Are you all right?"

I said, "Yes ma'am."

I stepped into the foyer remaining by the front door. She walked into her living room, turned around and saw me still standing in the foyer. She asked me to come into her living room. I did; she asked me to sit down. I did, as calmly as I could; I had never been invited in and sat in a white person's living room. She then asked if I would like to have a cup of coffee.

That really shook me. The thought flew through my mind that I was being set up. Again she asked me if I was okay. I told her that I was, it was just that I was new. I pulled myself together, skipped the coffee, took the report, and left.

I drove down the road, pulled to the side of the road and caught my breath. I later called my parents again to tell them that I actually went through a white person's front door. My mom warned again as she had more than once before, "Boy, don't let them kill you out there."

Later on that evening, I doubled up with a senior deputy to finish the shift.

One evening I was patrolling with a senior deputy, Ken Hansen. He told me of the Highlands Inn that was on our beat, and that we had to check on it periodically. It was located about four miles south of Carmel on Highway One. He said that as a teenager he worked there as a waiter.

A few minutes later, we entered the inn and saw the owner, Mr. Ramsey, standing nearby. He immediately recognized Hansen and walked toward us. Hansen introduced him to me, noting that I was also a pretty good singer. Mr. Ramsey asked that I come to the inn when I was off-duty and maybe see if I would be interested in singing a song or two in the cocktail lounge. I thanked him and told him that I had never sung in a cocktail lounge before. I also told him that this was the first time in my life that I'd been in an upscale inn. He smiled and obviously thought that I was making a joke but he understood when I explained my background. He told me that I was welcome to come to the inn any time, and that there was no discrimination at the Highlands Inn. It was a new and obviously very pleasurable experience for me. This was something else I had to share with my parents.

(Now I know you must be wondering how thick skulled I had to be for it to sink in with me that there could be a safe, happy life with integration. And as I said, it took a while to root out all the ugliness of the Deep South, but it took that long because it was really deep. It was protection, really, from getting hurt from doing something that violated the social code. You could get hurt. You could get killed. So it was a like a bullet proof vest that I was slow to remove.)

The following Sunday I was off-duty and I decided to go to the Highlands Inn for brunch. It was a wonderful time. I knew I could stop worrying about being called names or refused service. That wasn't going to happen here.

Afterwards I went to the cocktail lounge to listen to the pianist. He played the old standards and some Broadway tunes that I was familiar with. Just then Mr. Ramsey walked in and recognized me. He went out of his way to make me feel comfortable. I could not believe a white man could be so gracious.

Ramsey got up and played a miniature piano along with the pianist, who played a parlor grade. Mr. Ramsey talked me into singing a couple of show tunes. While singing, I noticed patrons coming from all parts of the lounge to hear me sing. I wasn't half-way through the first song when the area around me and the pianists was filled. There was not a seat empty. Each time I would finish a song, there would be loud applause. Among the audience were Susan Oliver and Jay Novello, two television celebrities.

The Highlands Inn has a fantastic view of the Pacific Ocean. Singing there that night – doing what I loved so much and had always wanted to do professionally – and enjoying the enthusiastic response from the audience, I felt like I was on top of the world. I never but in my wildest dreams thought that such a good thing could happen to me. And yes, I called my parents to tell them of this terrific experience.

I heard reports that some of the residents in rural Carmel Valley were trying to get me fired because they didn't want to discuss their problems with a black man. I wasn't going to get pushed out by them, so I made it a point to become known on a personal basis to some of the key people in the valley. Whenever I saw someone working or standing in their yards, I would get out of my car, walk over, and introduce myself. I knew that some people weren't used to seeing or talking with a black person, but I asked for a chance to let me serve them. As time passed on, I was invited to the different homes for coffee, lunch, dinner, or just to shoot the breeze. Before long, most were calling on me to discuss their personal problems. The buzz about me getting fired all but disappeared. It was very gratifying.

Once when I was in Cachagua, a very remote area in Carmel Valley, I was driving up the side of a ridge when I saw a boy, about ten years old, standing near the roadway. I stopped to talk with him. As I got out of my car, he ran up the trail and disappeared.

Later that day I saw him again. I told him that I was not going to hurt him, that I just wanted to meet him. He never uttered a sound; he just stared me like I was an alien who just got out of a spaceship. I extended my hand for a handshake. He walked towards me slowly. I could see he was confused. Instead of shaking my hand, he wiped the back of my hand with his to see if it was dirt. He thought that I needed a shower. I later learned that he had never seen a black man before. He could not figure out why I was dark and had kinky hair. That meeting turned out to be the beginning of a great friendship that continues to this day. Before long, these people I went out of my way to meet one on one were my back-ups whenever I needed support before other deputies could make it to the scene.

I had never come into contact with a black person in the vast Monterey County area except in Seaside. This was in part because so many blacks were either stationed at neighboring Fort Ord or lived next to the base after leaving the military. I patronized a Augustus Lewis' barbershop and a barbecue café there. I was called an "Uncle Tom" by a number of blacks there. That really hurt me. It seems as if I was caught between a rock and a hard place. Whites didn't like me because I was black and blacks didn't like me because I was "white." But they were the ones with the mindless prejudice.

One day I was in a room in our office. I overheard some deputies, in an adjoining room, discussing me. One said that

I could be reprimanded for things they would get fired for. I was nicknamed "Asbestos," because I could not be easily fired. Very funny. I did not like them calling me that name, but there wasn't anything I could do. I had to just think about that prejudice as sharpening me up like a whet stone.

I was told that Jim Tregea, Michael Hall, Van Pelt, and I would be attending the last police academy in Hollister in a few weeks. I could not wait to get there, because I wanted to meet other black peace officers and listen to some of their experiences.

Soon it was time for us to attend the police academy in Hollister. There were about 30 officers from around Northern California for a six-week training. I had expected to see a real fancy facility. Instead, it was a dump located by an old airstrip. Our sleeping quarters were in an old dilapidated single-walled building. We slept in bunks. It was very cold. The cafeteria was a dump as well, with two little old ladies doing the cooking and serving. The really disappointing thing was there wasn't even one other black peace officer there. I was the only one. If there was a good thing about the academy, it was we would go to a bowling alley nearby.

I got a kick out of Tregea and Hall arguing nightly about opening a window before they went to sleep. Mike liked the window opened for fresh air. Jim wanted it shut because it was cold winter air.

Jack Little, a retired Los Angeles zoot-suit detective, was in charge of the academy. He was in his late 50s, stood about 6'6" and was on the husky side. He told us stories about the old days, as in before search warrants and Miranda Rights changed a lot of what law enforcement is about.

Jack sensed that I might have been having problems acclimating. He called me into his office one day and we had a long talk. I told him that several times I had thought of resigning because I was so uncomfortable being the only black among all whites. It made it difficult for me to concentrate. I told him it had resurfaced again, there at the police academy, especially since I'd been looking forward to meeting other black officers. He urged me to stay and try not to let things bother me so much.

I did take Jack's advice. I put forth more effort and managed to finish the academy. To my surprise, I was elected president of the class. Yes, I called my parents to tell them the news. They were proud of their son.

# *Jail Duty*

About six months later my probationary period was over. I was called into the station commander's office. He said that some of the other deputies did not think that I would make a good deputy. Somehow, I knew this day was coming. But instead of firing me, the undersheriff took matters into his own hands. He extended my probation period and transferred me to the county jail in Salinas. I had seen other deputies do a lot of terrible things, but I had never ratted on any of them.

A short time later, the undersheriff asked me to come to his office. I was sure this time, I was going to be fired. But instead we had a very good discussion. He said that he knew what I have been going through as he had had the very same experiences because he was of Mexican descent. He asked that I hang in there as it was going to be tough for me being the first black deputy.

I worked the swing shift, in the jail with a group of deputies who seemed to be a decent guys. But I didn't let up for a minute. I did what I was told and worked hard to keep my job.

The county jail was a dated facility and had cells and doors made of Bethlehem steel. Nothing was high tech in those days. We had to open a large panel and turn a wheel in order to open cell doors. Felons were housed on the fourth floor; the misdemeanors on the second. On the ground floor was an office, a booking area, and a large holding cell. There were also cells adjacent to the holding cell in case we had to segregate unruly inmates. Lieutenant Ted Brown was the supervisor.

The women were housed upstairs and in the front of the building. Sergeant Betty Arnold was in charge there and she ran a tight ship. Anyone coming in raising hell got a good ass-whipping; unofficially, of course. Downstairs, underneath the Women's section, was the Records Division, where Gus Gustafson was in charge.

Attached to this building was the main office, which had the Civil Division and the offices of the sheriff and undersheriff.

It was In the military stockade where I first saw blacks, whites, Latinos and other races incarcerated. But this was the first time I had ever seen an integrated civilian county jail. I was also surprised to see some of the same inmates that I had in the Army stockade incarcerated in jail.

There was a large cell which we called the Bull Pen. Mostly weekenders were housed in there. Those were usually DUI'ers. I escorted a weekender to the pen. As I opened the large steel door to let him enter, I was pushed to the floor from behind by a Mexican trustee. I thought I was being ambushed but in fact the trustee saved my life. He had seen another prisoner inside the pen getting ready to strike me on the head with a heavy duty commercial broom. As the prisoner swung the broom, the trustee had pushed me down. The broom splintered into pieces when it struck the wall. It would have struck my temple and killed me.

I got up and wrestled with the prisoner and forced him in a nearby empty cell. When I returned to the front office, the other deputies asked what took me so long to lock up the weekender. It turned out the prisoner who tried to kill me was a drug addict and was probably high on something like pcp which causes violence and super strength.

Another time, the CHP dispatcher called the jail to

inform us that two officers were bringing in a father and son to the jail. The father was arrested for DUI and the son, also intoxicated, had assaulted the CHP officers. A short while later they arrived at the jail. Sergeant Crisan and I met them at the front door. We assisted the CHP getting them into the jail. They were robust and tough. Both said they didn't like niggers and I better not touch them.

Soon we had the both of them in the booking cell. As I was typing their booking sheet, the son kept spitting at me through the bars and calling me names such as "porch monkey," "jungle bunny," "nigger," and "spook." It was my first time hearing some of those names, and I had thought I'd heard them all. He and his dad were later sentenced to six months in the county jail and were housed in the same cell.

Each day, I would feed the prisoners and later give them their medication. Each time I would appear in front of their cell the son would again call me names and say how much he hated niggers. He would never eat the food I served him. He said that he did not like the idea of me having my hands on anything that's supposed to be given to him. Each time I passed his cell he would threaten me. I would look at him and give him the grin that the Cheshire cat had in the animated movie "Alice in Wonderland." This went on for a month.

Finally one day, I approached their cell. He saw me but did not utter a sound. I asked him if he was okay? He got up, walked towards me, and said, "I'm tired of hating you. No matter what I say, you just smile. You have been always good to me and my dad, making sure that we eat, and get our medication. I want to thank you." He extended his hand through the bars for a handshake. I shook his hand. When they were discharged, I was invited to their home. That really blew me away.

One night at 11p.m., I was leaving work and walking to my car (a '64 TR4) that was parked across the street from the jail. I noticed two Mexicans standing in front of it. I said, "Boy that sure is a nice car." One said that the car belonged to him and he was going to sell his friend the tires. Obviously they did not know the car was mine. I removed a revolver from my shoulder holster and told them, "That's my car, and in just a few seconds, I'm going to start shooting." They ran as fast as they could into the dark neighborhood. I know I should not have done that, but I had just purchased those tires the day before.

A few minutes later, I was sighing with relief but still nervous, because I thought they might follow me. They didn't. I lit up a Cuban rolled cigar, sat down in my car and strapped myself in a leather harness. This was before seat belts were mandatory. I was driving down the highway, when suddenly hot ashes fell between my legs and on the seat. My butt and the seat were on fire. I pulled over in a turnout with intentions of getting out, but couldn't unfasten the harness. I was yelling and screaming. I finally managed to undo the harness. My seat and the seat of my pants were burned. When I arrived at home, I sat in a tub of warm water, and then rubbed my butt with Neosporin.

Another night at the jail, a policeman brought a beautiful woman to the jail in handcuffs. I told him that he needed to take her to the women's facility in the front of the building. He ignored me. I told the policeman again that she needed to be in the women's section. Finally, the woman said that she is a man. I could have just died. He was wearing a woman's wig, a bra with tissue paper in it, and high heel shoes. The word got around the jail quickly, about the he-woman. Inmates on every floor were yelling, "Bring her up here!" I had to segregate her for her own safety.

## From Colored Town to Pebble Beach

One rainy night a bailiff, Wilbur House, was in a trial that lasted into the early evening. One trial was finished, but he had another one. He asked if a deputy could come from the jail to escort a felony prisoner back to the jail as they were done with him. I went to assist.

On our way back to the jail, the prisoner, who was handcuffed, and I were walking along and talking. He was black and he said to me that if I were white, he would run. I begged him not to even give it a thought. We walked into the foyer of the jail. I handed the paperwork to a deputy through a slot in a large window. The inmate was nearby standing in front of what we call "The Green Door," the inmate's entrance. I turned my head from him for two seconds. The inmate ran outside into the rainy dark night.

I ran after him in the dark rainy weather. I fired a shot into the air so my colleagues would know my whereabouts. There was a residential community near the courthouse area. I ran over there thinking he could possibly enter one of those homes. Instead I fell into a hole full of construction waste. My colleagues pulled me out of the hole. The prisoner escaped. I only had a few scratches, but I thought I would be fired in the morning, if not that night, for discharging my firearm.

The undersheriff was informed about what happened and asked that I come to his office early the next morning. I couldn't sleep that night. The next morning I walked into his office and placed my badge and gun belt on his desk. As I started to leave, he asked me to sit down. He said that I wasn't going to be fired. Was I surprised! He tossed my badge and gun belt back to me. He said someday that inmate would be apprehended and returned to this facility, or to the mortuary. His exact words to me were, "Don't worry about spilled milk. These kinds of incidents occur almost daily with peace officers throughout the nation." He told me that he had suspects escape from him a few times when he was a young peace officer. Boy, did I feel relieved.

That escape was the top news on radio and television. Each time I turned on the radio in my car, my name and details of the escape were being broadcasted. I did not come out of my apartment for three days. I was surprised at the attitude of the public about the escape. Most thought that I should have shot and killed him. Of course the guys in the office needled me about it for days. Some said they agreed with the public – that I should have shot him – but I think most of those guys were joking.

Another jail activity involved the state corrections department. Every month a large prisoner transport bus en route to San Quentin would stop at our facility. Prison personnel from the bus would lodge their prisoners in our jail overnight. The next morning their prisoners would be gathered along with the ones we had to transport to the prison.

On the second floor of the jail, there were empty cells. Usually illegal immigrants were housed in those. In one of those cells was a Mexican national. He had mental problems and so we kept him isolated. Each day, I would check up on him and talk with him. I really thought that we were friends, but we weren't. One of the deputies told me that while I was cleaning his cell, he was sitting on the upper bunk, with a shank in his hand. He told a deputy that he was about to stab me in the back of my neck when suddenly someone walked by and he put the weapon down.

I had worked the jail for almost a year and a half. I had seen murderers, scammers, child molesters, burglars, and every other kind of criminal. Just before I was to return to patrol, I had a great surprise. The undersheriff told me that the inmate who escaped had been captured and would be returned to our jail within a few days.

When the man arrived, he said that his escape was well planned. He had discussed the plan with a friend by phone at the visitor's jail. His friend was waiting for him a block away from the jail. They drove off immediately for Los Angeles. The handcuffs were removed shortly afterwards. He did not hang out after reaching Los Angeles; he knew he was wanted and did not want to be seen.

Later, he and his friends decided to burglarize an office located in a warehouse. They managed to gain entry but were unaware that they had activated a silent alarm. Minutes later, the LAPD surrounded the building. The burglars were told to come out with their hands up and surrender. The gang decided to make a run for it. They ran through the front entrance and into the parking lot, where the police were waiting. When they refused to stop, the police opened fire. The guy was hit in the right side of his body by a shotgun blast. He had a circular shot group of pellet wounds on the right side of his body, and another wound from a .38 caliber revolver. He spent almost a year in the hospital and was crippled for the rest of his life. But for what it's worth, and it was worth something to me, he apologized to me for all of the problems he caused me.

While I was working in the jail, the second black deputy sheriff, Jerry Cole, was hired in 1969. He patrolled with an instructor in north Monterey County. He was a very sharp individual who had just retired from the U.S. Army as a high-ranking enlisted Airborne Ranger. He didn't stay a deputy for long either, for some unknown reason. The third black sheriff's deputy hired was Ray Patterson, who is almost seven feet tall. Small world, I had been in the Army with Ray's father. He patrolled the North County area, as well.

# *Photographs*

**Great Grandparents**

**Monterey County Deputy 1978**

**Singing the National Anthem**

**With Rep. Sam Farr and Willie McCovey**

## With John Denver

## At the Salinas Rodeo

**Singing with The Conte Four**

## With Maya Angelou on Cannery Row

## With Clint Eastwood & Sheriff Norm Hicks

## With Les Brown and his Band of Renown

## With Ed Haber, Doris Day & Angie Dickinson

**With Charlie Sheen
on the set of "The Rookie"**

# <u>*On Patrol*</u>

It was around the time that I was attending the police academy in Hollister, and I still hadn't found a place of my own. I was still sleeping on a couch at my friend's house at Fort Ord when I met Carl Stephenson, a friend of their family. He was a new black teacher in the district and was looking for an apartment and a roommate. He asked if I would I be interested. I told him that I would be, and he could contact me at the academy by telephone. At the time, I had about two weeks left before graduation.

A few days later, Carl called and said that he found a nice two-bedroom apartment in a really nice neighborhood. The complex was composed of eight apartments. The only thing was that there were no black people in the area. Like me, Carl was also from the segregated South. I was glad he found an apartment, but was wondering whether our neighbors would be rednecks or just down to earth people.

After I graduated from the police academy, Carl and I moved into our apartment in the Monte Vista area of Monterey. We had a very liberal landlord and surprisingly neat tenants. They gave us a warm welcome. Most of the tenants were attractive white girls. You'd think that would be something a couple of young guys would appreciate, but Carl and I had mixed feelings. Being from the Deep South, we had an inbred fear about even thinking about a white girl. We wondered if we might have problems.

I loved to cook and had every spice needed for cooking. The girls always wanted to borrow just about everything including my vacuum cleaner. I would give them whatever they wanted.

After a few weeks, Carl and I began to feel at ease. There seemed to be no signs of racism among our neighbors. In fact, some of them would watch the news on television with us. They were open about their feelings that it was a shame the way blacks were being treated in the south. I never thought that I would ever hear that comment coming from a white person. It really felt good.

Only one of the girls was a slight problem. Every other day she would come into our apartment, whether she wanted to borrow something or not, to harass us. She was extremely attractive and knew it. Our sliding glass door was always unlocked. She would never knock, just walk in uninvited. She would always say that she knew that we wanted her, because she was beautiful and had an hour glass figure. She also said that she knew that we fantasized making love to her, but were afraid to admit it. I would always ask her to leave, as I was afraid the superiors in my office would hear about her and I could lose my job. But she finally got bored and stopped bothering us.

I decided to become a student at Monterey Peninsula College, a local junior college, in part because I wanted to meet new people, and there were some opportunities to advance myself. For instance, I wanted to study police science, and I also became a member of the chorus which got me back into music – the true love of my life. I became quite popular on the campus and in the community at large from my singing, especially as a result of being a soloist. I made a lot of new friends of all colors and nationalities. There were times when I would have a group of my new friends over for dinner. I was enjoying life.

One of the college choral members, a very nice young

white woman, lived in one of my patrol areas. She said that she and her family had seen me pass their house on numerous occasions. She asked that I stop in for coffee sometime. I did say that I would, but I never intended to. One day, I was passing their residence and I saw the family standing in the front yard. I blew my horn and waved as I was passing by. They waved for me to stop. I did, hesitantly. I met her parents and two brothers. They were very nice. They invited me to dinner, for whenever I had the time. And I accepted, somewhat reluctantly. This socializing with whites was still new to me.

One night, I was patrolling with a partner in Carmel Woods. Someone reported hearing screams, where a couple of females lived. We were nearby and arrived at their residence within two minutes. We did hear crying, screaming, and laughter coming from the house. We could not get in because a two by- four was bolted on the inside of the front door. We rapped on the door, but no one would let us in. We thought that we could get in through a window. These windows were really high. I put my partner, Ken Hansen, on my shoulders and raised him up to the window so he could see inside. He reported down to me, "Wow, these gals are cute, nude, and drunk." Ken said that there were wine bottles all over the floor and furniture. He added that they had prize-winning bodies. I said, "Hurry up, so I can see." He said, "Wait one more minute. Oh, they are fine." He said it was okay for me to let him me down so I could see for myself.

Then Ken lifted me upon his shoulders to the window. He had tricked me. Those ladies were very elderly. One, it turned out, was 77 years old and the other was 86.We managed to get into the house and then called a nearby relative to come to take care of them. I read my partner the riot act.

When I was patrolling in Carmel Valley on the swing shift, I received a call from a man who wanted to file a complaint against a neighbor. A few moments later, I arrived at his apartment and knocked on the door. He answered, looked at me and said, "You're a nigger. I don't like niggers."

I said to him, "I don't like niggers either." He seemed surprised and a bit confused by what I said.

"You don't like niggers either?" He shook his head and apparently changed his mind about making a complaint. As he closed his door, he was still scratching his head.

One swing shift, I was patrolling Marina and Sand City. In those days, there were two roadways, one going north, the other south. While travelling south going to Sand City, a blue '65 Mustang with a Louisiana license plate went speeding by me. A white man in his early thirties was behind the wheel. I tried to stop him in front of Fort Ord, but he ignored my siren and red lights. He finally stopped in the city of Seaside. He got out and said, "What is your problem, Boy?"

I reminded him that he was talking to a peace officer, rather than a boy.

"You're a nigger," he said, "and where I came from, you can't do anything to a white man!"

I told him, "You're in a different part of the world now, and you're under arrest." I wrestled with him and placed him into the caged area of my car and transported him to the Monterey Substation.

I was on swing shift still patrolling alone to better learn the area. This time I was in the Carmel area. I received a call from someone working at the Mission Ranch, reporting an unruly patron there. I arrived and spoke with the owner, Skip Heebner. He told me that there was an intoxicated patron standing at the waiters' and waitresses' station, preventing them from taking drink orders. He had been refused service because he arrived intoxicated. The man said that if he couldn't get served, nobody would. Heebner added that he didn't want to file charges against the man, he just wanted him to leave the premises.

I walked in and spoke with the subject. I explained to him that the owner did not want to file charges against him, he just wanted him to leave the premises. He said to me, "If I can't have a drink, no one else can." He continued to stand in front of the drink station. He said to me, "There is nothing you can do to me, Boy!"

Since he was uncooperative and refused to obey a legal order, I had to physically remove him from him from the restaurant and place him under arrest. I wrestled him out of the crowded restaurant and out to my patrol car. A little old woman opened the rear door to the caged rear seat for me. When it came time to face the charges, the man represented himself in court. He lost the case.

Sergeant Crisan, my supervisor, decided that I should ride with him. We patrolled Marina and Sand City that particular day. I learned quite a lot riding with him. I pushed out of my mind the notion I'd heard growing up that foreigners couldn't be trusted. With him it was easy because, as I said before, his manners were impeccable. He recounted to me how he and his immediate family had escaped from the communist regime in Romania to get to America.

Fort Ord was adjacent to Marina. A large number of soldiers lived there. There were a couple of bars there where someone could get into a fight almost daily. We had a list of names of the known troublemakers in Marina. John introduced me to some of the local residents and business people there.

We stopped at a local deli, where John bought spicy links of pepperoni. I had never eaten that before. He gave me a piece; I thought there was a fire in my mouth. My hair stood up like Don King's and tears came from my eyes.

John told me that in a few days we would patrol the Big Sur coast. We'd had reports that hundreds of people, many from Berkeley (a center of hippie activity) were planning to have a festival at Limekiln Creek campgrounds.

A few mornings later we drove down Highway One, about twenty-five miles south of Big Sur village. As we arrived at Limekiln Creek, we saw hundreds of psychedelically painted cars, buses, and trucks parked on both sides of the highway.

Limekiln Creek campgrounds are located underneath a highway bridge and borders the beach. We parked, looked down over the bridge and saw hundreds of people walking around in the nude. I had never seen anything like this in my life. A few other deputies arrived along with the CHP. Several tow trucks were hauling the vehicles away that were not parked properly off the roadway. The CHP was in charge of towing and accidents; the deputies handled penal code violations.

It would have been impossible to enforce any type of violations as there were thousands of people there. Some of the people were asking us to take off our uniforms and join them. Of course, we couldn't do that, even if we had wanted to, which we didn't.

There were lots of drug violations going on, but we were outnumbered and it would not have been safe to do anything about them.

Later on, a periodical called the "Berkeley Barb" had our

pictures on the front page, showing us walking among the people there. In those days, we were called "pigs."

We were down there for hours. A number of cars were towed away to the Big Sur garage. There were a number of unhappy people, when they found out that they would have to pay a substantial towing fee to get their cars.

On the way back, Sergeant Crisan told me he wanted to introduce me to a local resident who hated hippies. We stopped at his residence located about eight miles south of Big Sur proper on the very edge of the cliff. His place was about 800 feet above the ocean. Sergeant Crisan knocked on the door and this massive man answered the door. He was hairy like an ape and had the largest hands I have ever seen, a sub-bass voice, and as I saw later, he drank and ate enough for four men. He drank out of a flower vase rather than a regular drinking glass. He could eat a turkey for a snack. Anyway, he invited us into his house. His name was Walt Trotter, and he was a real live Paul Bunyan.

We sat down at his table and had coffee. He drank out of a small pail. Trotter told us that the locals had been talking of organizing a vigilante group. Trotter said that a number of the residents along the coast were tired of these trespassers. Trotter said that a few days ago, he saw a campfire with three people on one of his properties. He walked into the site and said, "The son-of-a-bitch that owns this property gets pretty pissed off when someone trespasses on his property." One of the campers said, "This is God's country." Trotter replied, "God hasn't paid his share of the goddamn taxes." He told us that he was afraid that he was going to hurt any trespasser that came on his property.

He had a cache of weapons in a nearby gun closet; more firearms than the entire sheriff's department. One of his favorite guns to shoot was an eight-inch barrel S&W. He said he never missed at whatever he was aiming.

I was introduced to Walt's brother who was equally as strong and had as big an appetite. During the summers, he would eat a large watermelon for a snack.

The sergeant also introduced me to some of the other Big Sur residents and business owners. This was quite an experience for me, as I had never seen real hippies – not the Berkeley types – before. These were people who had moved down to Big Sur many years earlier. I would have to say that they were real hippies, not just the weekend type that liked to dress up and do drugs. It was a real education going down to Big Sur.

I was back in Monterey on patrol a few days later when I received a call from a Catholic nursing home in rural Monterey, stating there was a disturbance there. When I arrived at the facility, a nun met me at the door and led me to the disturbance. I saw nuns being thrown out of a bedroom onto the floor of the hallway.

I ran into the bedroom and stopped the altercation. The patient was a little old woman who screamed each time one of the nurses (nuns) touched her. The patient's daughter was the one tossing the nuns out of the room. The daughter said each time the nurses would turn her mother over to bathe her, her mother would scream because the pain was excruciating. When she came to visit that day, she heard her mother screaming. She snapped and threw everyone out of the room. She apologized to the staff. No charges were filed against her.

There are two Catholic churches located on Highway One in the unincorporated area of Carmel that overlooks Monastery Beach. One of the churches is a monastery. No one ever sees the nuns as during mass and other services they are seated behind a grate. The nuns can still see the congregation. The church properties adjoin, but the nuns' order is separate from the other church.

The nuns at the monastery were constantly being disturbed by teenagers. The teens would come at night to try to peek in their quarters in an attempt to see the nuns. I later learned that they wanted to see if the nuns were bald. Each time the teenagers were outside peeking in the windows, the nuns would contact our office. By the time we would arrive, the teens were nowhere to be found. We had a number of such calls, but we were not successful in catching anyone because they could see us driving up the hill towards the monastery. They would run and hide in the thick forest behind in the hills behind the monastery.

One night, we received another call from the nuns. This time they told us to take our time as they had caught the teenagers. We arrived and were met by the Mother Superior who led us to the juveniles. There were six of them, all from Monterey, and they were lying on the ground tied up with rope. She said that she and the other nuns had been hiding in the bushes themselves every other night hoping the teenagers would return. That night the boys had sneaked onto the property, gone to the windows of the nuns' quarters, and tried to peek inside. The nuns surprised them, coming up on them from behind. The boys were wrestled to the ground by the nuns and tied up. All of the nuns were wearing their habits with hiking boots. Mother Superior explained that she had been brought up in China where she learned martial arts.

I had a nagging fear for longer than I would care to remember that I would be let go because there were too many people who didn't get like me. Not only fellow deputies, but also a number of attorneys from the DA's and Public Defender's offices. This I found out from a retired attorney. Apparently whatever complaints they had didn't hold much water with the sheriff since the only negative I got from the sheriff's office was a minor note I received on a monthly evaluation stating that I seemed to be more interested in studying music than police science at the college. That didn't seem real to me. I was just a member of the college chorus. No one ever asked me about it. And I <u>was</u> studying police science.

I bought a big horse named Ralph from Ray Hackworth, a well-known cowboy who had the September Ranch in Carmel Valley. Every other day I would ride in the hills or down to the Carmel River Beach for relaxation. A famous movie star, Kim Novak, and I used to ride together. She bred Arabian horses. Oftentimes, we would take a little girl, Lisa Johnson, with us.

I also rode in the Salinas Rodeo parade every year. It would start in south Salinas and end up in the rodeo grounds. At the beginning of the parade, a cowboy, Al Hansen, would stamp us on the back of our hand. Once one reached the rodeo grounds another cowboy, Harry Rhoades, would check the hand for the stamp. Once he saw the stamp we could continue to ride inside. I got into a hassle the first two days because I was so black the stamp could not be seen. I almost did not make it inside. I had the stamp put in the palm of my hand so it could be easily seen.

I learned that there was another Pat DuVal, who was a city policeman in Salinas. I could not believe it, but I finally met him, in person. He was a twin, even though he was a white male and a bit taller than me. We were always getting one another's mail and sometimes phone calls. Both of us participated in the Salinas Rodeo. We had fun confusing the public.

I continued to attend college and make friends. I was having the time of my life. One day a nice young white woman asked me to come to dinner at her home in Monterey. I made an excuse not to come. A few weeks later, her dad asked me to come; he would not accept a refusal. The fact that her father extended the invitation made it impossible to refuse, and I graciously accepted.

Two days later I drove to their house for dinner. I was a little nervous, but I tried to remember the table manners my mom taught me. As we were dining, the father asked if I had a girlfriend yet. I told him no. He said, "Well then, why don't you take Susan out?" I damn near died. I was speechless. For a white father to ask a black man to date his daughter was beyond anything I ever imagined. I lost my appetite and my mind. Susan was sitting next to me. She elbowed me and said, "I had to ask my dad to invite you to come here." We all laughed and I agreed to take her out.

After I left, I walked to my apartment up the hill; my legs felt like rubber. I could not believe what had happened. When I reached my apartment, I opened the sliding glass door and saw Carl sitting in the middle of the couch. I asked him to move towards one end of it, as I was about to faint. He asked what had happened. I told him. He asked the whereabouts of my car because he hadn't seen me drive up. I told him that I had driven it to Susan's house and forgotten it because I was so nervous.

Susan and I did date for a while. It was clean and wholesome. I allowed her to ride my horse while I was at work. I was a big step for me in realizing that not all the world was like the Deep South, that people of different races could getting along just fine, that the color of a person's skin didn't have to get in anyone's way.

During the latter part of 1970, I returned to the Monterey

Substation. This was at the new courthouse on Aquajito Road overlooking Highway One. The freeway was not open just yet; Caltrans was putting the finishing touches on the huge intersection with Fremont Street and Highway 68. The sheriff's office was located on the bottom floor of the courthouse building, along with the probation department, the county planning department, and the county supervisors' offices, plus the snack bar. The court rooms were upstairs on the second and third floors.

While I wasn't excited about returning to work with the same deputies who did not like me before, it didn't seem to bother me as much because I had a lot more time and good work experience under my belt.

Big Sur was still the place for "Flower Children" to come. Almost daily down there you could see old school buses that were converted into campers as were a bunch of old vans. Most were painted psychedelically. Many of the hippies wore Birkenstocks and only cotton clothing. In every other turnout on Highway One was one of their vehicles. There were quite a number of hitchhikers – thumb-trippers, we called them – up and down Highway One from Carmel to Big Sur and then south to Cambria, just past our jurisdiction in the next county. Among them were runaways from all over the world who had come here in search of something they hadn't found where they were.

Frequent complaints were made by property owners about trespassers. Some drove or camped on private property without permission. There was still talk about organizing a vigilante committee to deal with the trespassers. But communications for us had been significantly improved. A deputy no longer had to check in by using a public telephone. Towers had been placed on a mountaintop so deputies could communicate by two-way radio from the patrol car.

A gentleman from the San Francisco area had bought a new RV and planned to travel around the nation in it with his wife. A few weeks later, he had open heart surgery. After his recovery, he and his wife discussed their travel plans. They decided not to travel around the nation, but just on the West Coast. The RV had two gas tanks. He converted one of them into a waste tank. They decided to camp in the Big Sur campground and were resting comfortably. (You know what's coming, right?) About three in the morning, they were awakened by noises outside their RV. The man thought it was just deer or some other animals walking around in the bush.

The next morning when he walked outside to take a stretch, he saw two red jerry (gas) cans on the ground beneath the converted gas tank. The "deer" must have thought he was going to siphon gasoline from the tank as there was a piece of hose sticking in the "gas" tank. There was a stream of vomit leading from the RV to a nearby trail. The perp must have sucked quite a bit of waste into his mouth. I would have loved to see the look on his face when he got a mouthful.

It was 1968, and a year of tragedy. Martin Luther King, Jr. was assassinated April Fourth in Memphis by James Earl Ray. I was shocked to hear the news and then to see the coverage on television. To some whites, it was a laughing matter. But to the vast majority of Americans of every color, it was a real tragedy. Through the local coverage, I learned that the president of the Monterey NAACP was a white businessman. That was a surprise.

After the assassination of King, I received a number of anonymous calls telling me that Ray was in this area. Of course, it wasn't true. There were also several occasions when I was asked what I would do if I caught Ray myself. I'd look serious for a moment, then smile and walk away.

Arrangements had been made for me to sing for Robert Kennedy who was campaigning for the Democratic nomination for president. But he was assassinated by Sirhan Sirhan in Los Angeles in June. A song was written called "Mr. President" by a songwriter whose surname was Mitchell but I have forgotten his first name. The staff at the Highlands Inn had me rehearsing this number repeatedly. One of the people was a former Ziegfeld's Folly dancer.

Deputies would be assigned to a different beat every other day if not every day. That way we could learn the area and get familiar with some of the residents. One particular night I was patrolling with a partner in the Pacific Grove area. The PG Fire Department asked for assistance at a residence where several males were intoxicated. One of them was reportedly having a seizure, and someone had called for an ambulance. But some of the men were unruly and would not allow the EMTs and fire personnel to transport the man to the hospital. They were insisting that the man was okay.

We arrived at the scene along with backup deputies. As I walked into the bedroom, Lieutenant Ron Zeise of PG Fire Department was being threatened by one of the man's "friends." The guy said that he was going to get his shotgun and blow Zeise's brains out. When he started to reach into the closet, I put the barrel of my S&W .357 Magnum into his ear and said, "One false move and I will kill you so fast, you'll stink standing up." The threat – or promise – worked again. He suddenly had a change of mind. The man was transported to the hospital and some arrests were made.

Another time PG Fire had a call, this one involving a drastically over-weight woman who was having difficulty breathing. She weighed around 550 pounds. She was so big they could not get her out of the door. A heavy-duty chainsaw was used to cut a large opening in front of the house, and then a makeshift gurney was used to place her on the back of a pickup truck. She died before reaching the hospital. I wasn't there for this call; the story was told to me. I relate it because it's an example of how bizarre the work of fire and police really is.

One day at roll call, our commander said that someone had been racing on the closed freeway below our offices. He asked that we make area checks to see who was racing. He didn't know that it was us, racing with the CHP to see who had the fastest patrol car.

As I mentioned, I was studying police science at the college, where I got an Associate of Arts Degree. There was a number of peace officers taking classes at MPC. You could tell which of the students were law enforcement because we all sat against the walls in all of our classes. We all had some enemies among those in the student body.

Tor Spindler was one of our instructors. He was big in stature. So big he could not find a shirt large enough to fasten at the neck. He was tough but a nice man. We never missed his classes. Our other instructor was Dick Snibbe who smoked cigarettes while he lectured.

As I said before, I was a lover of Broadway tunes and classical music. Our college chorus gave a concert one evening. I had the privilege of singing the love duet from "Madame Butterfly" with Tamara Jacoubowsky, a great young soprano. We received a standing ovation that lasted for almost eight minutes. I could not hold back the tears. Her father was a very reputable architect and her mother was a sweet housewife. Her brother and sister were also nice. They all made me feel like family. I was very comfortable with them.

Dan Poole, who was a major in the U.S. Army, invited me to join the Monterey County Choral Society in Carmel. This group performed with the Monterey Symphony. Poole, who happened to be black, had been a member of this group for a few years. Rehearsals were held at the old Sunset Center in Carmel. The first rehearsal was a little unnerving because there were maybe a hundred members and only two of us were black. If I had any doubt that I would be accepted, it was quickly dispelled as I received a warm welcome from the members and the conductor, Haymo Taueber. It was absolutely heartwarming. Rehearsal was every Wednesday evening from seven to ten. I never missed one rehearsal. It made me feel every more at home here on the Monterey Peninsula.

Mr. Taueber auditioned me and told I was a counter-tenor. He had to explain to me what a countertenor was. I couldn't read music. I didn't really know much of anything about music, except that I could sing, and that singing had always been the most important part of my life. And it always would be.

(People ask why I didn't go back to Motown. It was because it seemed like there were new people, and I didn't think I'd fit in with them. Plus Motown had moved to Los Angeles and it was a different scene. I also thought that if I was to get into entertainment, I could do it with the connections from the people in Pebble Beach. If I ever I decided to go that way.)

In those days, the Black Panthers were quite popular, at least among blacks, especially in the San Francisco and Oakland area. One evening we were trying on our choral robes. I took my robe to another room because I was wearing a shoulder holster which had a small revolver in it. One woman happened to come in the room and saw my gear and screamed. She thought that I was a Black Panther. It was then I had to inform everyone that I was a peace officer. That was when I got the title of "The Singing Sheriff." It was a name given to me by Mr. Taueber.

One evening our college chorus went to Stanford University to participate in a huge concert. This was really heaven to me, especially as I was one of the soloists. I only wish my parents could have been there to see and hear me. I was overjoyed when there was a long line of people who wanted to congratulate me for doing a good job.

Mr. Taeber asked me to sing the countertenor solo, "The Roasted Swan," from Carmina Burana. Members of the chorus were thrilled to learn that I would be the soloist. I really felt comfortable, being a part of this group. It was like family. I could still hear my grandmom saying that I would be sorry, if I didn't learn to read music. She was right. Life would have been easier if I had known how to read music but that didn't stop me from enjoying what I did.

One day, Carl, an army Lieutenant named Ronald Valerie, and I decided we would go to the Santa Cruz Boardwalk. We were wearing suits that day. We stopped by one booth to toss a basketball through a hoop to win a prize. It was crowded on the walkway. It was my turn to shoot the ball. I was wearing my small off-duty revolver on my hip. I was unaware of it being visible through the vents of my suit. Suddenly, the crowd disappeared. We continued to play ball. A few moments later, we saw policemen were coming from both sides of the boardwalk towards us. They asked us not to make a move. One of the policemen said, "Wait a minute. I know him. He's Pat DuVal from the Monterey County Sheriff's Office. We went to the police academy together."

Boy, was I relieved. Dan Fite was the policeman who recognized me. They had gotten a call from someone who said they thought they had seen armed Black Panthers on the boardwalk. We left immediately afterwards, and everyone was sighing with relief.

One morning, CHP officer Tommy Pena and I were talking, while sitting in our patrol cars in a turnout just north of Carpenter and Highway One. Suddenly on our scanners we heard that the bank had just been robbed in Monterey at Soledad and Munras Streets. The suspect had left on foot headed towards the parking lot at the nearby Elks Club. He was attempting to leave the area in a black '65 Ford sedan that was parked in back of the parking lot. That was out of our jurisdiction, but we were close by. I said "Let's get in on this one!" Tommy said that he would go in front of parking lot, and I should come in the back.

The suspect was described as a WMA (white male adult), very thin, maybe 125 pounds, who had on a dirty denim jacket and jeans, a much-worn straw cowboy hat, and cowboy boots. He also was missing a few teeth, was wearing a red bandana, and he was carrying a .22 rifle.

We arrived at the parking lot within two minutes of the call. Tommy had him blocked in front and I in the back. Identification was no problem. The red bandana he used was hanging around the rearview mirror. Worse for him, he was trying to start his car by hot-wiring it. We got out of our cars and drew our pistols and ordered him to get out of the car. He came out peacefully. We took him and got the rifle out of the car. He asked with a heavy southern drawl, "What do ya'll want me fer?" Just then, the Monterey Police arrived along with witnesses from the bank.

One of the policemen said, "That's the guy I helped get his car started yesterday." The suspect's car was extremely dirty and so full of junk there was no room for a passenger. The trunk was tied down with rope. We retrieved the Hefty bag that had the bank's cash in it.

There was an apartment building on the west side of the parking lot. A couple said they were eating breakfast on their balcony at approximately ten that morning when they noticed the old black car stop in the large and empty parking lot. They saw the suspect get out of the car and place a rifle on his shoulder. He slowly walked down the hill. They had thought that was strange, but didn't think to report him to the authorities.

Someone in the bank later told the police that he saw the robber driving through the drive-in teller lane outside about 9:50 that morning. The bank tellers reported that the suspect entered the bank at approximately 10:15; that he was wearing his red bandana on his face, but it kept falling around his neck. He had a Hefty bag in his hand and the rifle in the other. He said good morning to the tellers in his southern drawl. He asked them to put the cash in the bag and told them that no one would get hurt. He was very slow and clumsy, according to one of the tellers. He left the bank very slowly; didn't seem to be in a hurry. He almost tripped going out of the door.

The suspect was from the rural area of West Virginia. He said he was broke, hungry, and needed gas money. I told him where he is going he'd get meals three times a day and he wouldn't need any gas, other than what the food gave him. I told him in a sarcastic voice that if he should ever decide to rob another bank, he should have a fast vehicle to leave the scene. I told him he would want to steal a Porsche next time. The guy didn't know what a Porsche was.

I was patrolling in the Carmel Valley area one evening. At approximately 9:30, a Del Mesa resident reported a disturbance. This is a high-end 55+ retirement community, and a very nice place to live. I spoke with the reporting party, an English woman, who introduced herself as a Dame. She lived in a townhouse near the clubhouse. She said that she had been trying to read, but could not concentrate because of the loud music coming from the clubhouse nearby. I was listening to the music as she was speaking. It didn't seem loud to me at all. I explained to her that this was private property, and that this matter should be discussed at the next association board meeting. I also told her that I would speak with whoever was in charge about her problem.

I went to the clubhouse where a dance was being held. The band was made up of five male residents of the community. They were playing "Tuxedo Junction" when I entered. I explained the situation to an 84-year-old woman who was in charge of the affair. She became upset and asked that I stick around for a few more minutes. When I asked why, she said that I might have to take her to jail because she is going to "kick the shit out of her." The Dame had apparently been a problem since she moved in, she said; no one liked her. I managed to talk her out of assaulting the Dame. I didn't think she could have assaulted her anyway, as she was very frail and used a walking cane.

One day, I received a call from a resident of another retirement community in Carmel Valley. I met with the caller at her residence in this community. She said that she had been assaulted by another resident there. Her arm was black and blue. At one time, she lived in another condo next door to her assailant. She had moved to the other side of the complex to keep from coming into contact with the woman. Even though she lived on the other side, she liked using the laundry facility near her former residence.

At approximately eleven that morning, she was doing

her laundry and her former neighbor saw her and asked why she was using that laundry room since she had one on her side of the complex. The complainant told her that she liked this one better. The former neighbor, who we'll call Mrs. A, told her that she did not like her and that she needed to gather her laundry and use the facility on the other side. The caller refused. Mrs. A slapped her on the arm. The caller became frightened and ran out with Mrs. A in pursuit. Both ran through the complex to the clubhouse. There they ran through the beauty shop where a Japanese woman was the beautician. Mrs. A stopped chasing the complainant momentarily, went over to the beautician, slapped her and said, "That's for my husband, who was wounded in Pearl Harbor."

I spoke with Mrs. A who volunteered that she had assaulted the caller, and I told to leave her to leave the woman alone. No charges were filed.


One night, I received a disturbance call from the dispatcher at a trailer camp that was located in an unincorporated area of Monterey County. I was to contact the owner whom we'll call Mrs. Doe. The dispatcher said that there had been many disturbance calls reported from that camp. Some in law enforcement referred to it as "Dogpatch," as it was a bunch of old, dilapidated cabins and trailers. This was my first call there.

I arrived at the camp shortly thereafter. There were beer cans and liquor and wine bottles scattered on the ground and the area overgrown with weeds. The real estate was in need of repair. Most of the residents there were very unkempt. Most had only a few teeth. Some were annoyed because a black man – yours truly – was on the premises.

Mrs. Doe, the owner, was a white woman in her 60's. She walked up to me and said, "You're a goddamn nigger."

She said that she has never liked niggers and told me to get my "black ass and badge" off the property. I told her that I came to answer a dispatch call and that I was not offended by her name calling. But because she refused to cooperate, there was nothing I could do so I left. Later I discussed the matter with my supervisor. He said I handled the situation correctly.

One rainy afternoon, two sedans collided at the busy intersection of Highway One and Carpenter in the unincorporated area of Carmel. I was nearby and heard the crash. I arrived just moments later, and noticed one of the sedans was on its side. I got up on the side of the sedan, opened the door and entered slowly. There was a slightly obese woman who seemed to be in her late forties. I assured her that everything was going to be alright. I said we would have to hurry to get her out of the car because there was a possibility of the sedan catching afire and exploding.

She looked at me and said, "Don't touch me."

I said to her, "Lady, we don't have time to waste."

She said, "I have never been touched by a nigger before. I can get out by myself."

You might think I was ready to just back off and let her die in her car, but the truth was that I had heard this nonsense all my life, and I pretty much blocked it out. Besides, her racial ignorance was not going to get in the way of me doing my job. Meanwhile, the CHP and fire personnel had arrived on the scene and they helped me get her out. Her injuries were not life threatening.

Another night, I received a call from a resident who lived on the beach in the unincorporated area of Pacific Grove. The caller wanted to report a trespassing problem. The caller's home was an old Spanish-style two-story home that overlooked the ocean and sat on several acres. I arrived at the home and knocked on the door. The owner, a tall white man in his late seventies, opened the door. He looked at me and slammed the door in my face. I turned around and started to walk to my patrol car. I was going to contact my supervisor about what had happened, when the man opened the door and asked me to come inside. Once I was inside, I noticed he and his wife were hoarders. There was trash, books, and periodicals stacked in every room. The stench was absolutely gross. One had to walk around the edge of a room. He told me that he was in the John Birch Society.

Instead of telling me about his trespass complaint, he was trying to convince me that Martin Luther King, Jr. was a communist. I told him that I was only interested in his complaint to the dispatcher. He said that he didn't want to discuss his problem with a black. I was glad to leave that house.

It was time for deputies to patrol the Pebble Beach area. This was a very affluent and upscale community. In those days, there were four gates manned by security guards. People had to pay a fee to enter and to drive the Seventeen-Mile Drive, where there were some of the most expensive homes in the world. Some residents are CEO's, retired politicians, business owners, celebrities and others who had considerable wealth. Residents paid a twenty-five dollar road tax annually and received a metal shield that was placed on the grill of their vehicle. I was a bit nervous working there because I had heard that blacks and a few other races were barred from buying property there. I never did see any blacks, except for a few domestic workers.

The Pebble Beach Company owns the roads, hotels, shopping malls, and the golf courses. Back in the days, the Bing Crosby Pro-Am Golf tournament (now the AT&T

Pebble Beach National Pro-Am) and the Concours d' Elegance vintage car exhibition were two of the most famous events held there annually, and still are.

Some of the residents could not believe a black deputy would be patrolling in Pebble Beach. Some did not want to discuss their problems with a black person. One woman asked if I would use the service entrance rather than come to her front door. Another asked if I could park my patrol car down the street and walk up to her house. She did not want her friends to see a patrol car in front of her house, let alone a black man climbing out of it.

Whenever I would be in the vicinity of the Spyglass Golf Course, I would stop for a moment to watch the golfers hitting their balls. Watching them fascinated me because I had never seen a driving range before.

One day, Frank Thacker, the golf pro at Spyglass, saw me watching the golfers. He asked why I didn't come out to play some time. I told him that I did not know how to play. In fact, I'd never been on a golf course in my life. Where I came from, I explained, black people were not allowed to play golf. He said that he would teach me. I declined the offer and told him that I did not want him to lose his job. He asked how he could lose his job. I told him if he is caught teaching a black to play, he'd probably lose his job. That's the way it was in the South. He said he didn't care about what went on in the South. Just give him a time that I could come for my first lesson.

So after that, my roommate, Carl, and I came out every other day for a lesson. As a trade, we would gather the balls that were hit on the driving range in buckets and bring them back to the pro shop. I was having the time of my life. Around the time of my first golf lesson, I also started learning to play tennis at the college. Tennis was another sport that hadn't been open to blacks where I grew up.

As time passed, most of the residents I encountered accepted me. I found myself being invited to dinners and other events. My fears and doubts were losing their power over me.

A Hollywood producer, Frank Bauer, heard me sing at some event and came up to me afterwards. He said that he thought that maybe I could become an actor. He asked me to speak with his brother, Jack Bauer, who was the Head Casting Director at Twentieth-Century Fox. He said that he would call to tell his brother about me. I had been a sheriff's deputy for about three years then.

Three weeks later, I spoke again with Mr. Bauer who said that he had spoken with his brother in Hollywood about me and that I should go meet him. I drove down to Hollywood and spoke with Jack Bauer. He said that he would get an agent for me. He telephoned an agent, Lil Cumber, and asked her to represent me. She agreed to do so. Afterwards, we talked more about me. He asked how soon I could move to Hollywood. I asked him to let me give this some thought and I would call him.

My mind was not made up. Driving back from Los Angeles to Monterey, I was thinking really hard about my next move. I could not believe the connections I had made.

Two days later, I was riding my horse with my celebrity friend. We were riding towards Carmel via the Carmel River. I told her about my interview. She asked, "How long have you been a sheriff's deputy?"

"Almost three years now," I replied.

She said to me, "Hollywood is in a slump now. It's hard for me to get a decent role. Right now, what few roles for blacks there are seem to be going to professional football players, like O.J. Simpson." Then she said, "You're eating regularly, aren't you?"

"Yes," I answered.

"You like your job, your salary, and you have health insurance?"

"Yes," I agreed.

"And you can't very well play the part of Daniel Boone." Then she laid it out for me: if I had an agent, I would be sent to read for parts. There could be a number of people reading for the same role. Maybe I would get it but more likely I wouldn't. I would still have to eat that day.

That really gave me food for thought, so to speak, since I was cooking and eating at home. I decided that this was not the time for me go to Hollywood.

I was on patrol in Carmel Valley on a cool Sunday when someone reported seeing a nude WFA (white female adult) sitting on a hillside amongst tall thistles. I borrowed a large shirt from a nearby resident to put on her. I asked her to come to me out of the thistles; she kept looking upward towards the sky. It was overcast so I don't know what she thought she was looking at.

I used my handy-talkie to ask the Carmel Village EMT's to come out since the woman seemed to be mentally unstable. My instructions to them were to drive out quietly and park behind my patrol car. They were to bring out their gurney and have it ready once she had turned her back on me and I could corral her.

The woman seemed to be in a daze. As she approached me, she turned around in front of me. I put the shirt over her. She asked me to put my arms over her shoulders and hold her hands. While she was facing the opposite direction and I was standing behind her with my arms over her shoulders holding her hands, I nodded to the EMT personnel. They came up the hill with the gurney. Just then, she looked into the clouds above and said, "Lord take us now." As she was speaking, there was an opening in the clouds; the strong rays of the sun began to shine on us. I am not superstitious, but I was beginning to wonder if she had some kind of power. She kept asking the Lord to take us now. I kept saying, "No, Lord, no." The gurney was right behind me. I quickly pulled her down on her back onto the gurney, and the EMT people strapped her down. She was then brought down the hill and transported to the Crisis Center at Community Hospital.

Afterwards I learned the woman was reported missing from Fresno. Her vehicle was located on Laureles Grade, parked in a turn out. I also learned from a Carmel Valley realtor that she had walked into their office the day before. She had just walked in, said nothing to any one, drank several cupfuls of water from their water cooler and left.

There are times when a peace officer cannot get a backup. However, when it was mentioned that the woman was nude, everyone wanted to come and assist.

During the latter part of the summer of 1970, I decided to visit my parents in Florida. They had moved into a new home and I was anxious to see them. I flew into Orlando's Airport, rented a Lincoln Town car, and headed for their new home which was also in Fort Pierce. (I rented these large cars so I could drive my mom, our relatives, and friends around.)

When I left the airport, I made it a point to engage the cruise control at 55 mph. I was driving on I-95 highway, when suddenly I was pulled over by a sheriff's deputy. He asked to see my license. I asked him why I was being stopped. He said he noticed this car was a rental and asked my permission to search the trunk. I refused to allow him to do so; he seemed surprised. I asked him why he wanted to search the trunk. He said because most black guys rent large cars to mule (transport) dope. I told him that I hadn't committed any crime; therefore he could not search the vehicle.

I was somewhat nervous about not letting him search the trunk, because I remember the times when blacks were assaulted by crooked peace officers; some who belonged to the Ku Klux Klan. He was perturbed. He looked at my driver's license and asked what I did for a living. I told him I was a deputy sheriff, and a pretty well educated one. He said that I'd gone to California and gotten uppity. A few moments later, I was free to go on my way.

Uppity was not a word I used to describe my life in The Golden State, but I sure shocked my parents, relatives, and family friends when I told them how it was for me in California. They could not get over me being the first black sheriff's deputy in Monterey County. Nor could they believe I was the only black person living in Carmel.

I told them about the restaurants, how I had no problem being served at any of them. I told them about the beaches as well. They were not segregated at all. I had never seen a "Colored" or "White Only" sign. Theaters, drive-ins, and other public facilities were not segregated at all. If I saw an empty tennis court anywhere, I could just go out and play with no problem.

Schools were integrated and had been for many decades. I told my mom about the hospital where blacks and whites were being treated by white and black doctors. There was no such thing as a colored ward there. EMT's transported every race to the hospital.

I went on and on about how my life was, and I could see in the faces of some of them that they were having a hard time believing what I was saying. I also told my parents that when I retired I was going to get my own restaurant so we as a family can dine together.

Another day there I took my Mom shopping. I told her to choose anything she wanted and I would pay for it. We went to a very high-end woman's boutique. A white woman said to us that this store was too expensive for coloreds, that there was a much cheaper store in another mall nearby. I told the woman that whatever my mom wanted she could have. I could afford to purchase anything there. In fact, I was thinking of buying the whole block, destroying all of the buildings and making a nice parking lot. Her face turned red. We left without buying anything.

After spending quality time with my parents, it was time for me to return to Carmel. The visit was nice, but things had not changed that much in Fort Pierce. There was talk about integrating schools. The way it was going to be done was by bussing.

While I was there, I told my parents, relatives and friends about the legendary Walt Trotter, the human Paul Bunyan who lived in Big Sur. No one believed me when I told them how much he and his brother, Frank, ate at one sitting and how strong they were. I told them if ever they came to visit, I would take them to his house. My dad thought that I had gone crazy and that I just said those things about the Trotters for laughs.

Before I left home, there must have been at least a dozen peace officers from various jurisdictions at my parents' house who came to see me off. They were all teared up, as I was. I really hated to leave my former classmates and friends. I had gotten jobs for some of them, but none of them wanted to associate with white people. They were from the old school.

As I was flying back to California, I was thinking of what my parents went through during their lifetime, and how where I now lived was another world. I knew for a fact that they had never been in a real restaurant or enjoyed going to a concert. I wished that they would have come to with live me and enjoyed a better life.

My roommate, Carl, decided to move to Seaside so he could be closer to the school where he was teaching. Larry Fitzwater, my next door neighbor, had a roommate who was being transferred to another bank branch, so Larry and I became roommates. Larry was a really nice white guy. He was the manager of a Wells Fargo Bank in the local shopping mall. We never had an argument.

Larry never ate in restaurants or ate anything I cooked. He was a country boy and hunter. He had a storage locker filled with deer hearts and venison. He was a very frugal person. He drove a red 356 Porsche coupe. We had a lot of fun.

One day the captain asked me if I had ever thought of going into the detective division. I told him that I had on occasion, but being the only black guy around, I would probably get be mistaken for a burglar and be shot and maybe killed. He thought I was joking and laughed. He said everyone seemed to know me. I told him, "Yes, when I'm in uniform I'm recognized, especially in the daytime. At night, it's a different story."

He suggested that I try it for a couple of weeks, and that I should wear civilian clothes and use the unmarked sedan out back to contact victims of burglaries and other crimes in the Carmel area.

I agreed to do so. A couple of nights later I was in civilian clothes driving the blue sedan checking the neighborhoods. It was very cold that night. I was wearing my old "Columbo" overcoat.

I decided to call on a close friend who'd been burglarized twice in a month during the night. I usually had coffee with him at his house or his office.

He had a walkway with solar lights that led from the street to his front door. I stepped onto the walkway and he saw me coming towards his door. I thought he recognized me. Instead he came and met me with a baseball bat in his hand and said, "You came to rip me off again, you son-of-a-bitch, huh?" He began swinging the bat at me. I turned around and started running down the street. We both were running, but he was right behind me trying to hit me with the bat. I was trying to get my ID out of my back pocket, but I couldn't. I yelled at him, "It's me, Pat Duval!"

He said, "I know Pat DuVal. He is a close friend of mine. You are the one who has been ripping us off." We ran from Hatton and Third Streets to Ocean Avenue. Just then, the headlights of a car shone in my face; he saw me and said, "Oh Pat, I had no idea it was you. I couldn't see your face in the darkness." We were both out of breath and held on to one another until we reached his house. There we had a few cups of coffee and had sort of a laugh about it.

After I left, I thought to myself that what happened was exactly what I had told the captain I was worried about. I didn't think I was going to like this very much. A few nights later, a caller reported someone trying to break into her residence in Carmel Woods on Valley Way between Guadalupe and Carpenter streets.

I was nearby and happened to know the caller. I arrived before the patrol, got out of my car, ran up to the front door and knocked. The female caller was screaming from upstairs. She said, "Get away from my door. I've called the sheriff already and they will be here any second now to get you."

I said, "This is Pat DuVal. I'm here to help you."

She said, "I'm not coming downstairs, besides you don't sound like Pat DuVal to me." I told her that I would come inside through the window beside the front door. I raised the window, got my head and chest through the window and was suddenly being struck several times by the woman with a broom handle. She said, "This will teach you not to break into my house, you bastard." Just then the patrol arrived. An officer told her who I was. She couldn't stop apologizing as she held my head and washed the blood from my right ear with a wash cloth. I was lucky she didn't strike me on the temple.

Another night, I was sitting in a residential area watching for anything suspicious. Several cars went by but I didn't see the suspect that I was trying to apprehend. Just then, a caller reported seeing a black man sitting in a blue Plymouth sedan. The caller said that there had been several burglaries occurring in this area and that was probably the suspect. I immediately called dispatch and told them that it was me.

Another night, I saw a '74 Cadillac parked on the south side of the freeway with its hazard lights activated on. I got out to assist the driver. I walked up to the driver's side and asked if I could help. She looked at me and screamed, "You're going to rob and rape me." I showed her my ID and told her that I was a sheriff's deputy. Finally, she calmed down, but she had scared the living daylights out of me, just as I had apparently done to her.

One night I was checking a suspicious vehicle that was parked on the north side of Highway One near the artichoke fields in Carmel. Someone reported that a black man was attempting to break into a vehicle parked along the road at the artichoke fields. The deputies arrived and saw it was me again.

After several more such embarrassing moments, I decided to go back into uniform where I felt considerably more comfortable. This detective crap was for the birds, I told the captain, saying if this had been the Deep South, I would have been lynched long before they discovered I was a peace officer.

One morning in Big Sur proper, a sedan struck two or three cars parked along the roadway. A witness reported it and said that there were two white males in the vehicle. The driver had sped away heading north rather than remaining at the scene. A thorough description of the vehicle was given.

Moments later, a CHP officer and a deputy sheriff stopped the suspects at the Little Sur River. They had the suspects and ordered them to place everything in their pockets on the hood of the patrol car. The driver placed the contents of his pockets on the hood which included funny looking bones. The deputy asked, "What kind of bones are these?"

The suspect said they were chicken bones. The deputy said that he was from Oklahoma and lived on a farm and had never seen chicken bones that looked like those. The other suspect pleaded with his accomplice to please tell the truth about the bones. The suspect hesitated for a moment and then told them that they were human finger bones. The officers thought he was trying to be smart at first, but then the suspect offered to tell the story about the bones.

He said that he used all kind of drugs. They were so powerful, he said, they had made him cannibalistic. He said that he and his friend were hitchhiking on the side of a highway in another state (Colorado or Montana) and were picked up by a male college student. They decided after a long drive to camp near a stream just off the highway. The suspect had taken all of these drugs while they were camped. Later that night, he got up and killed the student, dismembered him, and eaten parts of his body. The torso should still be at that campsite, he said. He kept the finger bones for a snack. The vehicle they're driving belonged to the victim.

The sheriff of that county was notified. He and some of

his deputies went to the site. Sure enough, there was a decomposing torso in that area. The judge dismissed the hit and run case against these suspects and had them returned to the state where the homicide occurred. This story made the *National Enquirer*.

One day I was patrolling the Big Sur coast about 65 miles south of Carmel. A local informed me of a large Ford sedan that had five occupants standing around it, about ten minutes further down Highway One. It seemed they were having trouble. I drove about five miles south into an area where there was no radio communications. I found the car and I asked what kind of problems they were having. No one said a word. They just stared at me. I asked again. Still no one said a word. Finally, one of the gentleman said that they were from South Africa and had never seen a black with authority before. Their problem? They had gotten out looking at the scenery and the steering wheel had locked. It was a rental car and I unlocked the steering wheel for them. The three men and two women were really grateful and wanted to take photos of me with them.

One night I was on patrol with a partner, Wilber House, on the Big Sur coast. We were about thirty-five miles south of Big Sur proper when we saw a woman who had run out of gasoline for her Volvo coupe. As we were driving her north to get gasoline in Lucia, it started to rain. On the way back to her car, it began to rain heavily.

As I was driving, the headlights of my car shone on a backpack that was on the edge of the cliff. I got out taking a quick look, but seeing no one in the vicinity. I picked up the pack and placed it in the trunk of our patrol car. My intentions were to take it to our office and place it into our evidence locker. That was if we couldn't find the owner beforehand.

We returned to the Volvo, put five gallons of gas in it and got it started. Moments later, the woman was on her way home. We returned to the area where the backpack was found. I kept asking myself why was it there. It was really pouring by this time. I turned on my powerful spotlight and aimed it downward towards the ocean. I thought I heard someone yelling for help. It was not only raining heavily but the wind had come up and it was difficult to hear. But I told my partner that I could swear I heard someone calling for help! My partner watched and listened as well. Each time I aimed the spotlight towards the ocean, we both heard a voice crying for help.

I called the dispatcher and asked to have a rescue team respond as quickly as possible. Then I used my bullhorn to tell the subject to hold on as it was going to be a while before help would arrive. Soon a CHP car arrived. The officer tied a harness around himself and to his front push bumper and went over the cliff. He heard the man who was trapped underneath a ledge, but he could not reach him. A little more than an hour later, the rescue team arrived. With the use of the specially-equipped truck, they rappelled over the side of the cliff, and brought the man up to safety.

The fellow said that earlier in the evening he was sitting on the edge of the cliff watching the sunset. Suddenly the place where he was sitting gave way. He rolled all the way down the cliff to the beach and the high tide line of the ocean. He spent hours crawling up the mountainside, trying to get back to the roadway. He had to stop because he crawled underneath a ledge and could not get out from underneath it. He knew his chances for living were slim. He said that when he saw the spotlight, he yelled as loud as he could for help. He was lucky to only have bruises and abrasions. He was very lucky that when he'd gone down the cliff his backpack had been left by the side of the road and picked up in our lights. Otherwise he never would have been found; at least not alive. He was taken to CHOMP for examination. He never stopped thanking us.

There was often labor unrest in our heavily agricultural region. A number of times I was involved in keeping the peace. There were two incidents worth reporting, one with a worker and another with an owner.

The first was when a Mexican woman said to me that she did not like niggers. I never thought I would hear that coming from a Latina. I thought she would know very well about our history of oppression as she had suffered the same. But she went on to say that blacks were dirty and they stole. I was out of line and I knew it. But I told her that I was a very rich man, that I planned to buy up most of the farms in the area, and then I planned to build townhouses and condos on the properties, and green them with Astroturf. There wouldn't be any farm labor or landscaping jobs for anyone.

Later, I was in the office of one of the growers with a group of other ag(riculture) company people and some other law enforcement people. He was telling us some of the problems he was having with striking farm workers. For some unknown reason he used the phrase, "There's a nigger in the woodpile." Seconds later, he ran over to me and apologized repeatedly. Actually, I had never heard the saying before.

No matter what is said by the public, a peace officer is to remain peaceful and not respond as he might feel like doing at the time. He must maintain the peace.

At some of the locations of labor unrest, the strikers would go out of their way to cause problems that could wind up becoming dangerous. For instance, at one camp the strikers were known to scatter twisted nails in the roadway, therefore causing tires to go flat. At other camps, eggs were thrown at us.

We were dealing with such tense situations in the Salinas Valley for months at a time. We were supposed to be in that area to prevent trouble. A crowd was expected to gather in the area about one in the afternoon. All of the officers were walking to their positions. I could not move because of an excruciating pain in my side. I didn't know it at the time, but I was suffering from an appendicitis. The guys kept yelling for me to come with the rest of the group. But suddenly I fell to the ground. Two detectives were in the area. They put me in their sedan, placed the magnetic blue light on the roof, and drove off to CHOMP some forty miles away. I wasn't there when later that day some workers were killed by a train passing through Chualar.

We got there in less than an hour. I had asked the detectives to call my roommate, Larry Fitzwater, and have him meet me in the emergency room there. The detectives left me in the ER and moments later Larry arrived. The doctor asked Larry to rush me to the Escaton hospital in downtown Monterey as all of the operating rooms at CHOMP were being used.

Our apartment was nearby. I asked Larry to stop by there so I could put on some clean underwear. Larry was reluctant, but he stopped there anyway. I was in pain still, but at least my underwear was clean. When we arrived at the hospital, the nurse told me that another nurse would be coming in to prep me. I was lying in my bed between two older gentlemen who were also in pain. Both were asking the Lord to take them away. When the nurse came in to prep me, I recognized her right away. I had stopped her on the freeway for speeding; I didn't write her up, but she had been mad at me. I started calling on the Lord, along with the other two old guys, though with a different request. I wasn't ready to die.

I had been in the department for a few years, but I never had the desire to get promoted. In my case, I just felt lucky to be there. I did take a promotional examination, but did not pass. Someone from the inside said that I passed and that I should check for sure. When I asked about those records, they could not be found. What was I to do? I dropped the matter, rather than risk getting fired for making waves.

I continued to work on the Monterey Peninsula, where I was still known as "The Singing Sheriff." I was quite popular, in those days. I sang the National Anthem at many entertainment functions, and at both professional basketball and football games. I sang at countless weddings, funerals, and fundraisers. I continued to perform with the Monterey County Symphony, and in later years, I performed with I Cantori and the Monterey Peninsula Chorus.

I met a retired politician, Jack Westland, in Pebble Beach. He was a great golfer. In the twenties and thirties, he had won many amateur golf tournaments. He asked me to come to his residence for a meeting. I agreed to do so.

Later that week I met with him, and there were some other businessmen and politicians present as well. I was really curious about this meeting. He said that they had all been watching me and listening to me sing. They had also noticed how well I got along with people. Jack said he had spoken to Governor Ronald Reagan about me, and Reagan had written a letter to Mr. Westland. Mr. Westland thought that I should be working security in the White House.

One day I got another call from Jack Westland, asking me to meet him again at his residence in Pebble Beach. The next day we met. He said that he is in the process of arranging a meeting between me and President Nixon. He had convinced the president that I would be a very good asset to his Advanced Party Staff. I could not believe what I was hearing. He said that he would let me think it over. It only took me a moment to think. I told him that I would accept the job. The Secret Service, unbeknownst to me, was already doing a background check on me.

A few days later, my landlord, Jack Currier, said that Secret Service agents were asking questions about me. I was only hoping that the sheriff's office would not be contacted. Not yet; I wanted to be the one to tell them that I was leaving.

I continued to do my job as a deputy, and kept wondering whether I would be doing the right thing in taking a job with the White House. I was told to wait a while, as something very newsworthy was going to be happening soon. I later learned that it was the resignation of Spiro Agnew, the Vice-President of the United States. He had been involved in a Maryland corruption scandal.

I was again asked to wait for a while because a close friend of Mr. Westland was going to become the Vice President. Of course, we later learned that he would be Gerald R. Ford. The Veep, as Mr. Westland called him, was coming to Pebble Beach and wanted to meet me. He did come here and we met. Later, whenever President Ford came to the Peninsula, he always took time to meet with me. He would stay at Darius Keaton's home or Leonard Firestone's on the 17-Mile Drive in Pebble Beach.

By now this was 1974 and Mr. Ford, then the Vice President, said to me that he was going to be in California for a few days, and then going to Hawaii in April. Air Force One would be parked at the San Francisco International Airport. He asked if I was willing to travel with him. I told him, "I'm ready." He planned to use the motorcade to go to Stanford as he had to make a speech there. The following day he would be speaking in Fresno, and then he would come to Pebble Beach. Afterwards, he would go to Hawaii to make another speech and that I was welcome to come along if I would like to. I was elated.

I did not discuss these plans with anyone. I continued to do my job as a journeyman patrolman.

I received a call from Jack Westland who asked that I meet him at his residence in Pebble Beach. He told me that the Vice President had to cancel the plans made for April. He said, "Tell Big Pat to hold on for a while longer, as something very serious is happening in the White House." Now I was wondering what was going on. I knew about the Watergate Scandal but I had no idea that it would wind up bringing down the President. Mr. Nixon announced his resignation on the night of August 8, 1974. The next day, Nixon left Washington, and Gerald Ford was sworn in as President of the United States. Amazing, and also amazing was the fact that President Ford kept in touch with me.

I met with him from time to time. He asked that Ansel Adams and I meet with him at the St. Francis Hotel in San Francisco. A funny thing happened to me while I was sitting in the lobby, waiting to see the President. The bellman was walking and calling my name aloud. When I told him that I was Pat DuVal, he looked at me and said, "Don't be funny." I was livid but cool. I showed him my ID and he apologized to me.

Shortly afterward I met with the President. We talked more about the job on the Advanced Party Staff and he introduced me to Red Cavaney, the head of the staff. I spoke with Red and also was introduced to some of the Secret Service agents. We kept in touch, as Red would call my office in Monterey or at my home. I still could not believe what was happening to me. I was just a small town black kid who had never been around white folks.

President Ford pardoned Richard Nixon. People were very upset about that and said that they were not going to vote for Ford the next election. I was doing some serious thinking about my future, too.

I met with the President again in Pebble Beach. I told him that I had given the matter a lot of thought. I told him I decided to remain in my job as a deputy sheriff in Monterey, but would certainly help him in any way I could. I told him that I would have the people here purchase copies of his book, if he would autograph them. He agreed to do so. I had access to a '74 Cadillac sedan that had a large trunk. Each time he would come I would have books for him to autograph. This worked out very well. Had I had a B.A. degree, I probably would have had the confidence and sense of security to leave the sheriff's office, and try a new path since my connections were very strong in Washington, D.C.

As we all know, President Ford lost the 1976 election to Jimmy Carter. After the swearing-in ceremony, President Ford took his final trip on Air Force One for a visit to Pebble Beach. When his plane landed at the Monterey Airport, I was waiting at the bottom of the ramp for Mr. Ford. The door to the plane opened, and he waved at the large crowd, saw me and said, "Hello Pat." I was the very first one he talked to when he exited the plane. The news media had reported that I said, "He remembered my name!" That was absolutely false.

We continued to keep in touch. He recommended to the former governor and soon to be president, Ronald Reagan, that he offer me a position in his organization.

Though I never moved to Washington, I remember some very gratifying moments. There were times when I would overhear people asking, "Who is that black man who's with the President each time he's here ?" I even walked with President Ford and Hale Irwin at the AT&T Golf

Tournament in Pebble Beach.

In 1975, I received a call informing me that my mom was about to undergo open heart surgery at Mount Sinai Hospital in Miami. I went to the Bank of America, to purchased $350 in traveler's cheques and $250 in fifty-dollar bills, and boarded an airplane for Miami.

When I arrived, Mom was undergoing surgery. I asked my kid brother to have lunch with me in the concession downstairs. It was a buffet. The white patron ahead of me paid for his lunch with a traveler's check. I had cheques also and decided to use one as well. I approached the cashier with the cheque. She told me that they do not take traveler's cheques.

I said, "I just saw you take one from the guy ahead of me." She said again that she was not going to take my cheque. I was furious, but tried to look calm. I gave her one of my new fifty dollar bills. She asked, "Is this a good fifty dollar bill? It looks like it's counterfeit to me."

I'd had enough."Who is the owner?" I asked her.

She asked why I needed to know.

I told her, "Because I'm going to buy this place this afternoon and you will not be working for me." I used a credit card to pay for lunch. I found out later that she was always rude to minorities. I never went back to that concession. This was more than a decade after the Civil Rights Act had been signed into law and this depravity was still common in the Old South.

One evening, I met Jim Lange, the host of the television game show, "The Dating Game," at a popular hangout in Carmel. We were discussing the possibility of blacks becoming game show hosts someday. I told him of the dilemma I had a while back with 20th Century Fox. I was sorry I did not take a chance on becoming involved in the movies, but I did not think I would have a chance.

He thought that it was about time for the networks to have a black game show host. He actually arranged for me to have an interview in Hollywood, with a very reputable agency that handles the top game shows. I was so excited.

A few days later, I went to be interviewed. The owner of the agency himself interviewed me. I thought that was just great. But he dropped the hammer on me when he said that while he believed that I was capable and could do the show host job, because I was black, he would not be able to get a sponsor for me. He used Nat King Cole as an example. Cole had a television show for a while, but could not get sponsors because he was black. Big sponsors do not make money with black celebrities. I could have just died. He wished me luck. I thanked him for the interview and walked out to my car.

I sat in my car for a while crying and pounding on my steering wheel. A little white woman who was walking her dog stopped and asked me if I was all right. With my face covered with tears, I told her I was all right. I was so outraged at being turned away because of my race. When would we end this insanity?

I used to visit my friend, Gerald Schroeder, a music professor at the Golden West College in Costa Mesa. During the summers, he conducted the Disneyland Orchestra in Anaheim. Through him, I met Patti Page and Leslie Uggams, among others.

I later met Alf Clausen, music director for the TV show *The Simpsons*, and the late Tommy Wolf. We all became good friends. They all thought that if I relocated to Southern California I could perhaps become a successful singer and actor. I guess I didn't have enough confidence in myself at that time.

After living in Monterey for a few years, I moved to the Big Sur coast to live upstairs over the Rocky Point Restaurant. It is located twelve miles south of Carmel and overlooks the ocean. The owners of the restaurant, who lived in the Carmel area, asked me to live there for security reasons. In the past, several thefts and burglaries had occurred there after closing.

I had a female Doberman Pinscher I had gotten as the result of a divorce case. The couple did not want her to go to either of them so they gave her to me. She was very well trained and responded to verbal commands as well as hand signals.

Each morning, I would let her out to run around the large property. The restaurant was open Tuesday through Sunday from 4 until 10 and closed on Mondays. The prep man would come daily to set up for dinner. There was a gate on the highway that was locked. Each delivery service had a key to the gate. From the gate to the restaurant was a few hundred yards downhill.

One morning at about 8:30, I was in my apartment drinking coffee and watching the fishing boats out on the ocean. I looked down in a grassy area near the cove just to the south of the restaurant, and saw a WFA with long red hair lying face down writing on a pad. She was naked.

I went down there and asked her what was she doing on the property, and in the nude. I asked her name. She said her name was Mother Nature, she was writing a book, and this area seemed to be the best place to write. Her clothes were in the brush nearby. I thought that I was going to have problems with her but I was relieved that she didn't cause a fuss. I asked her politely to leave the area which she did.

An old rancher had complained to a deputy about trespassers camping on his beach property. They had erected an

Indian-type teepee and are were living in it. They chased him away when he attempted to confront them. The deputy, Bob "Rock" Batson, who was a large man in stature, told him not to worry as he would take care of the matter.

This particular deputy was known to be strongly anti-hippie. And he was known to carry a razor-sharp machete.

Early the next morning, this deputy brought a rookie deputy with him. In order to get to this privately-owned beach, they had to park their vehicle on the highway and walk about a quarter-mile down to the beach. The deputy had the rookie walk with him to the edge of the cliff. There they could see the large teepee down below. He handed the rookie a rifle with a scope. The rookie asked what he was supposed to do. He was told to keep an eye on the patrol car up on the highway and to watch him down below. If anyone should try to attack him down below, the young colleague was to shoot them.

The senior deputy later claimed he could not find an opening to the teepee. So he stepped back, swung that machete downward into the side and made an opening. He stepped inside and said, "Good morning," to about a dozen trespassers who had been sleeping. The deputy informed them that they were trespassing and had ten minutes to get everything they owned off the premises. Anything that was left after ten minutes would be cut into little bitty pieces and they would have to "police up" each piece. The deputy sat on a rock nearby, checking the time on his watch. Ten minutes later, he ripped up everything in sight with that machete. One of the trespassers asked the deputy why he was doing this to them. He put his hand on the trespasser's shoulder and said, "Son, consider me as urban renewal." It took more than an hour for them to clean up that area.

A trauma doctor lived a few miles south of Rocky Point

on Highway One. He worked at a hospital in the San Joaquin Valley. He rode a motorcycle to work on Monday and came home on Sunday. This particular Sunday, he came home on his motorcycle very intoxicated. He knocked on the door. When his wife opened the door, he fell face down on the floor. She managed to drag him to their bed, but she was furious at him.

After a while he had sobered up somewhat. He asked, "What's been happening?"

She was really mad and replied, "You silly son-of-a-bitch. Every Sunday, you come here drunk and I am tired of it. It's the only time you are home with your family!" She said, "I'll tell you what has happened. Our neighbors were here visiting and sitting on the couch. The goddamn boiler blew up in the basement. It blew a hole in the floor underneath the couch, where the guests were sitting and blew them out of the house onto the ground. Other than that, nothing's happening." She slapped him around for a while, and then he called me to quell the situation. By the time I arrived, she had quieted down.

One afternoon, two lesbian cowgirls were sitting at the Fernwood Bar in Big Sur drinking, hugging, and kissing. The restaurant was in the same room. The bartender asked them to "take it outside" as there were children watching. One of the women asked the bartender to fix them another drink. He refused. She said, "Then I'll fix it myself." She proceeded to walk behind the bar. The bartender attempted to stop her, but she struck him in the face with her fist. Another one of the employees came to assist the bartender. The other woman joined in and the fight was on. They broke bottles of wine and liquor, glasses, and everything else behind the bar. Someone called the sheriff's office. The women left hurriedly in a '73 TR4 heading south. The CHP was attempting to apprehend them as well.

About three miles south of Fernwood on Highway One there is a very sharp curve in front of another restaurant called Nepenthe. The driver was going too fast and could not negotiate the curve. As a result, the car rolled over in the large gravel turnout. The car was upside down on top of one of the women. A big strong tourist who was standing nearby when the car turned over, pulled a fence post out of the ground. He used it to lever up the car so she could be pulled out from underneath. We arrived just then.

As we were getting out of our patrol cars, both of the injured women tried to attack us. The ambulance arrived and we wrestled to get them on a gurney. They were then transported to the hospital, and later booked for assault.

A Big Sur businessman told me that he had been having a problem with a Flower Child who had been pan-handling in front of his business. Each time he asked the man to go elsewhere, he got the finger. He described the man to me. I told him that I knew who he was talking about.

A day or two later, I saw the man he had complained about. I told him, as I had countless times before, to stop panhandling in front of these businesses. He just laughed and walked away.

A few days later this same panhandler was standing in front of an eatery. A little old couple was about to walk into the establishment to have lunch. The panhandler asked for money to buy a sandwich. The little old woman called him a creep and told him that he needed to get a job and then he would have money. The creep reached into the opened tote bag she was carrying, grabbed a five dollar bill, and left laughing. This angered the couple. The thief went out on the roadway and began hitch hiking. He was wearing prescription dark shades, his long hair was pulled back into a ponytail, and he was very unkempt in his appearance.

Instead of eating lunch, the couple got back into their van. They drove down the highway and turned around. According to a witness, the little old woman was hanging out of the window, swinging what seemed to be a bank bag full of coins. When they drove up to the hitchhiker, she hit him in the face with the bag, knocking him out cold. They stopped for a moment. She got out and removed the five dollar bill from his hand. They then turned around and headed north on Highway One.

I arrived on the scene about a half-hour later. I'd had been on another call about ten miles south. The guy was dazed. He glasses were broken, and his face was bleeding a bit. I got the details of what happened from the guy and a witness. I told him, "Justice was served." He left Big Sur for good a week later.

There certainly were some characters in Big Sur during the Seventies, and that's an understatement. One was nicknamed Band-Aid. Each time he would pass a utility pole or a tree, he would think it was a woman. He would curse the tree or pole, call it filthy names, and slap it with his hand until he bled. Afterwards he would put a band-aid on the cuts and go to the next one. One day I saw him slapping a pole, and I said, "Don't hit her anymore, Band-Aid. Let her go." I must have gotten through to him in some way, because he would sometimes say to the tree, "You better be glad Pat was here. Otherwise, I would have killed you."

There was another character who carried a long florescent light bulb in each hand. He would stand in the middle of the highway and try to light them by trying to get a charge from the sky.

Another was Indian Mike who was always drunk and slept in trash bins. He also liked to sleep in the middle of the highway. I don't know how he stayed alive.

Tommy Thompson, another homeless man, told me that he didn't give a damn about eating. Just give him a bottle of Strawberry Hill wine and he was satisfied. He and his friends lived in dugouts (nests) in the side of an embankment overlooking the ocean.

One time when there were fishermen out fishing from their aluminum boat three miles from shore, one of the fishermen saw what seemed like a body floating in the kelp. It was Tommy drunk and floating on his back. They tried to pull him into the boat, but Tommy started to fight them. He was so drunk, he did not realize he had fallen into the ocean.

A bunch of these guys was drinking wine in an old cabin in Gorda one night. One of them fell asleep while they were all drinking and talking. Finally, they all fell asleep. They were all huddled together to keep warm. The next morning they had all awakened, except for one. They shook and slapped him trying to wake him up. But he was dead and stiff as a board.

Many years ago, a tough gal named Diana Frame owned the café and store in Gorda. She was a straight shot with a crossbow. Her boyfriend, Roland, was always pulling pranks on people. Early one morning, Roland got a gallon of wine out of the store. He somehow wired it up with piano wire. He placed it at the edge of the turnout, very close to the road, covered the wires up with gravel and plugged it into an electrical outlet in the store. There was a guy thumb-tripping (hitchhiking) outside. A truck stopped to give him a lift. He asked the driver to wait for a moment, as he had to grab his bottle of wine. He grabbed that bottle and was almost electrocuted. Roland was inside the store laughing.

I remember when the Gorda café was leased by a French couple in their late seventies. When they first bought the café, she cleaned it so well that one could eat off the floor. The wife did not like Flower Children. Customers would have to knock at the door, and she would open a little slot like in a speakeasy to see if it was a real customer like a clean-looking tourist and not some grungy local. Only people who were neat and clean were permitted to come inside.

The couple was not liked by the locals who did everything to upset them because they were no longer allowed to come into the café, which they had been by the previous owners. One night, some of the locals went to the front and pressed their faces against the front window, making ugly faces. It frightened the old man who was very sickly. He grabbed a .38 revolver and, fed up with the constant harassment, threatened to shoot them. He had Parkinson disease and shook. The locals were outside the door banging on it, making noises, and faces on the window. The wife took the gun from him, went outside, and shot one of the locals in the leg. They left in an old pickup truck so fast that they forgot to pick up the man that was shot. They returned, picked him up, and tossed him in the bed of the truck, and fled.

Charges were filed against her; the court took her gun away, and she was placed on probation. She told the judge that she would shoot again if she was harassed by the locals.

In 1974, a movie called "Zandy's Bride" starring Gene Hackman was shot at the Post Ranch in Big Sur. Mr. and Mrs. Post owned the ranch, which was thousands of wilderness acres on which they ran cattle for more than sixty years. Each year, we would celebrate their anniversary. Mr. Post would always play his accordion. We really had a lot of fun there.

As the book had been written by a Big Sur local, the movie company that had bought the rights decided to shoot it in Big Sur. They decided that the Post Ranch was the ideal spot in which to film the story.

One day while filming, a trained Bear (Gentle Ben) was being used in a scene. The Bear had been drinking beer and was misbehaving. Eight trainers were trying to pull the bear with a device called a lunge to where the scene was to be filmed. The lunge was attached to headgear worn by the bear. Each time the bear was tugged, he would jerk his head, therefore causing the trainers to fall down to the ground. Walt Trotter was operating a Caterpillar tractor nearby. He asked the trainers if they would like some help. They gladly accepted.

As noted earlier, Walt is a very large man. He asked them to give him the lunge. He told them they could sit down and rest. One of the trainers said that Walt was crazy and was risking his life by trying to handle the bear alone. Walt tied the lunge around his big hands and pulled the bear towards him. The bear jerked his head backwards probably thinking he was going to make Walt fall to the ground. Instead, Walt pulled so hard the bear fell to the ground dazed. Walt looked into its face and slapped him up side his head. The bear got up, and they shot that scene with no problems. Each time the bear would see Walt, he would back away.

I mentioned Walt Trotter was big in stature. I stopped by his house later that evening. He was eating. On his table was a giant bowl of salad, a long loaf of French bread, twenty-five pieces of chicken, fourteen artichokes, a half-gallon of milk, and a pie. He had already eaten his snack, a small turkey.

Someone came to Walt's house one day and told him that some hippies in an old school bus were camped on some property he care-takes. Walt went up there, grabbed the bus underneath and tried to push it over the cliff. The occupants were inside screaming and pleading with him not to push them into the ocean below. He gave then thirty seconds to move out. They got out even faster.

On the Peninsula, an old cowboy had been evicted from his residence. During the last days, he went to an auction in Castroville and bought an old nag. He put a bale of hay in each room of the house, filled the bath tub with water and locked the horse in house. A couple of days later, the new owner of the house came and could not believe what he saw. The horse had pissed and pooped all over the house causing more than $25,000 in damage.

I got the surprise of my life, when I was given a cameo role, in a movie called *The Enforcer*, starring Clint Eastwood, Harry Guardino, and Tyne Daly. What an experience, being in a "Dirty Harry" movie. This was filmed in 1976 in San Francisco.

Paige Abel and I were in a scene together. In real life he was a deputy sheriff of Alpine County, as well as being a friend of Clint Eastwood's. We portrayed detectives. We had cameo roles and I was in a scene with Clint Eastwood. Having this part allowed me to join the Screen Actors Guild. Our scene was filmed in the police station on Bryant Street in San Francisco. (The best part of all of this was eating. In those days, I could really eat.)

Deputy Hank Klaput was patrolling in Pebble Beach. A

woman called to report that her two black boys had been kidnaped from her home in Pebble Beach. I was working in rural Carmel Valley when I heard him get the call. I said to myself, "How nice. Someone in Pebble Beach adopted two black boys and now they've been kidnaped. That's really too bad." Funny, I had never seen nor heard of these boys. I couldn't wait to hear the details from the deputy. I spoke with Hank later and he said the boys were two black jockey statutes that were standing at her front gate.

In nearby Pacific Grove one Sunday afternoon, a realtor was showing clients a residence in the dunes area of Asilomar. While walking through the living room area, a faint cry for help came from the fireplace. Everyone looked at one another to see whether they heard anything. Sure enough, everyone heard it again. The realtor knelt down into the fireplace, looked upward into the chimney and saw a man, who had planned to burgle the residence, stuck inside. The man pleaded with the realtor to get him out, telling him that he had been in the chimney since the Friday night. He could not have gotten into the house anyway because of the damper.

One morning at Rocky Point I had just awakened, when I heard the sound of shotgun blasts. It seemed to have been coming from the mansion across the highway. I quickly put on my clothes and rushed over there because a widow lived there alone. I quickly drove up the long driveway to the house. As I was getting out of my car, there was another shot. I found her standing in the doorway wearing a blue down robe. I yelled at her, asking what she was shooting at. Her answer: "I'm pruning my tree." She didn't want to hire anyone, so she shot the limbs off.

Her next door neighbor was also a handful. She often

claimed that she was being raped repeatedly by aliens through mental telepathy. I told her to make a hat out of heavy-duty foil and wear it. That it would keep the aliens away. I don't know if it worked, but she was happy I had helped her.

The gate at Rocky Point Restaurant was closed until dinnertime at 4 p.m. Every other weekend, the same soldier would park on the highway and walk down our driveway to the ocean to fish. We got to be friends. He said he had to feed seven children and they all loved fish. I showed him how to open the gate to get to the area where he fished but that he would have to be gone before the restaurant opened.

For a long time it worked out fine. One night I came home at midnight and saw his van still parked and locked on the property overlooking the cove. I turned on the cove lights, went down, and called for him. I got no response. I called his home at Fort Ord and asked his wife about his whereabouts. She said he had never come home for dinner. I immediately reported it to my office and told them that a rescue team was needed. I could not sleep all night.

Our rescue team and a Coast Guard helicopter were on the scene at daybreak. The helicopter flew the area off the cove just a few feet above water. They saw his fishing tackle and other accessories below on the rocks, but there was no sign of the fisherman. The search lasted most of that day and then for several days afterward but without any luck. He was never found. His wife said he did not believe in banks, and that he might have had $10,000 cash on his person. I was interviewed several times by officers of the U.S. Army. The family had planned to file a lawsuit against me for facilitating his disappearance, but they changed their minds for some reason.

I recall one funny story that involved my mother, who lived in Florida. I became friends with the actor, Doug McClure. He lived in Pebble Beach. My mother loved to watch "The Virginian." She even watched all of the reruns. She could almost recite the actor's lines. She only knew Doug as Trampas, his character's name on the television program. She never knew his real name. I was home talking to my mom on the telephone one morning when Doug stopped by.

I told her that the actor who played Trampas in "The Virginian" had just walked through the door. She asked if she could say hello to him. I asked Doug to go to the other phone, as my mom would like to say hello to him. He picked up the phone. Mom said to him, "I love you to death, boy. Why can't you stay out on that ranch and do your chores? I get so mad when you get in fights in that dirty old saloon. Now behave yourself."

"Mom, this is just a television show. He's only acting," I told her.

"I don't care," she responded, "I don't like anyone putting their hands on him." She died still loving Trampas.

My dad used to ask friends who were coming out to California to "check up on me." Especially he couldn't believe my description of Walt Trotter. But I introduced some of them to Walt, and when they went back to Florida, they told him what I had told him was true about this Paul Bunyan in real life, and his amazing appetite.

My parents came out to visit me when I had my stroke but I was okay. Then they came again, and they were so surprised because there were all these white people here who knew me. We were standing on the corner of San Carlos and Ocean in Carmel, and people were stopping and saying "hi" to me. My mom said, "Boy, wait 'til I tell the girls at home there's all these white folks coming up at talking to you. And all these kids grabbing you by the leg and hugging you. You know, we've been here an hour and a half on this corner."

My brother's been out here a couple of times, too, but my sister hasn't been able to come out. She has a special needs kid so she can't. She lives with my dad in Fort Pierce. My dad is 95. My mom died in 2002.

# *The Entertainer*

For a few years I had been at the Highlands Inn singing every other weekend. The pianist then was B. J. Thompson. During the seventies, Mr. Ramsey passed away. His widow, Patricia Ramsey, asked me to think about singing in the cocktail lounge. I told her that I didn't have the experience entertaining like that. She said she would give me $75 for singing from 7 to 10 on Friday and Saturday evenings. Plus I could have all I wanted to eat and drink. Seventy-five dollars in those days was a lot of money to me. I told her that I would be willing to give it a try. It turned out to be a great success because each weekend I would sing to a packed house. I sang until the inn sold around 1982. Ted Roe was my accompanist. He looked exactly like the KFC founder with white hair, beard, and moustache.

Shortly afterwards, I was singing on a regular basis at Laureles Lodge, in Carmel Valley. I was there for a number of years with my accompanist, Steve Tosh. We filled the place every night. The first weekend there were over three hundred people who came out to hear us, but they couldn't get in because the lounge only had a capacity of fifty. But there were many times when we packed a little more than a hundred in there. I was there for years and made many friends.

I had a great time at Laureles Lodge. People – even some whom I had stopped for speeding or some other offense – would come to sing-alongs with me.

In 1983, Clint Eastwood gave me another cameo role in

a hit movie he was making called *Sudden Impact*. Most of this film was shot in Santa Cruz. I portrayed the courtroom bailiff. I had the opening dialogue in this movie. Sandra Locke was the co-star.

In 1986 I was picked to do another cameo role in a movie called *Quiet Cool*, starring James Remar. It was an action movie in which I portrayed a detective. It, too, was filmed in the Santa Cruz area. It did not make a hit on the circuit like Eastwood movies.

In 1990, Eastwood gave me another cameo role in the movie *The Rookie*. My part was shot in Los Angeles in the L.A. Times building. I had the opening dialogue in this movie as well. Charlie Sheen co-starred in that one.

Eastwood was concerned about my health. He did not like to see me eating a lot of fatty foods. We had a choice of foods while filming this movie. I decided to eat two large New York cuts of steak, potatoes, and other unhealthy foods. I also got a plate with salmon and vegetables in case Clint decided to eat lunch along with us. I did not think that he would sit with us because there were so many actors eating. There were two long tables for actors to sit and eat.

But Clint did decide to eat with us. One of my lookouts said, "There's Clint." I had not taken a bite out of the steak yet. I took the plate with the steak, placed it in the seat of the chair next to me and pushed the chair under the table. I placed the salmon plate in front of me. Clint decided to sit in front of me. I never got to eat the steak. He always checked my plates at functions or restaurants. He was looking out for me because I had had a stroke.

I suffered a stroke one night after attending Clint Eastwood's first reception as Mayor of Carmel in 1986. When he was elected, he joked that he thought he had the black vote all tied up, until he found out I lived five houses outside of the city limits.

While recovering, I hosted a television show for one year, called *Saturday Night Twilight* on the local Monterey CBS affiliate. This was opposite NBC's blockbuster *Saturday Night Live*. I had two hours. I would show three half- hour episodes of *Twilight Zone* and a half- hour of something else.

I also sang "I Love You, California" at the California Rodeo in Salinas for the first time. I had a stroke back around that time but I wasn't going to miss it for the world. I went on stage using crutches. I was the fourth person in 85 years to sing the state song at the rodeo, and I have been singing it now for the last thirty years.

I also hosted a police show called "Crime Stoppers" on that CBS affiliate. It was like the show *America's Most Wanted*.

KSBW, the NBC affiliate in the market, tried to launch a show called *Around Town with Pat DuVal*. It was a community calendar type show which never got off the ground.

At this point, I would like share some of the other musical performances I have participated in.

I hosted the AT&T Kick-Off (formerly the Bing Crosby Clambake) from 1990-93. There I sang with a number of celebrities such as the Gatlin Brothers, Charlie Daniels, Vince Gill, Glenn Campbell and his daughter, Debbie, B.J. Thomas, the Smothers Brothers, and the late Phil Harris.

I sang the National Anthem at Candlestick Park in San Francisco at the Giants baseball games a couple of times. Bob Lurie was then the owner of the team.

I would also fly to Houston, Texas, to sing the National Anthem at The Summit Arena before the Houston Rockets basketball games. Charlie and Kittsie Thomas were the owners of the team.

I was still performing with the Monterey County Symphony and the Monterey Bay Symphony.

In 1995, I participated in a fundraiser called "The Flood Relief" along with Clint Eastwood, Paul Anka, and Coach John Madden. The Carmel River had flooded and caused extensive damage to homes and land from Carmel Valley to the mouth of the river at Carmel Point.

There was a celebrity tennis match called "The Challenge" held in Pebble Beach. I sang the National Anthem there as well.

I was also considered to sing the National Anthem for President Clinton's second inauguration.

Rosemary Clooney had me as a guest at her "The Betty Clooney Foundation" fundraiser at the Dorothy Chandler Pavilion, in Los Angeles. There were forty-eight stars participating including Bob and Delores Hope, Carol Channing, Bea Arthur, Ray Charles, Beverly D'Angelo, Suzanne Somers, Peggy Lee, and Natalie Cole. There we had the Singers Salute to the Songwriters. Jerry Herman was one of the honorees.

I have done a number of commercials as well. They were shown in other parts of the nation though not here on the Monterey Peninsula.

I had the first Cabaret style show at Spanish Bay Resort in the restaurant that is now known as the "Stix." Steve Tosh and I played there on weekends from 8:30 to 11p.m., back when Tom Oliver was president of the Pebble Beach Company.

I remember one night we were playing at Spanish Bay. While singing, I could hear someone choking. There were four people eating dinner to my immediate right. An elderly woman was turning blue. She was choking on a piece of meat. I tossed my microphone down, pulled her from the chair and did the Heimlich maneuver on her. The piece of meat shot out of her mouth across the floor of the room. She thanked me for saving her life.

My audience was not only composed of the local residents, but famous politicians, CEOs, pro-golfers, and even astronauts. Alan Shepherd was a regular.

I think I mentioned that I sang with Les Brown and His Band of Renown. I received a call from a public relations man late one Saturday night. He said Paul Anka was to perform with the band for a political function, but had an emergency and could not make it. He asked me if I could take his place. I told him that Les Brown would not play for a small shot like me. Besides, I had to patrol Carmel Valley.

The next day, while I was on the Carmel Valley patrol, the sheriff called me on the radio and asked that I call him by telephone. I called him a few minutes later. He said that he received a call from a public relations man asking that I replace Paul Anka at a fundraiser. He was supposed to perform with Les Brown and his Band of Renown at Quail Meadows. The sheriff asked me to sing in his place, as it would be good public relations for our department. I told him that I didn't think Les Brown would play for a "nobody" like me. Then he told me that Doris Day had made the arrangements. I asked if I should change my uniform and go out in civilian clothes. He said not to change clothes; just go in uniform and take the patrol car. He wanted me to go immediately.

I went to the site where the fundraiser was being held. When I arrived in the patrol car, some people thought that something unlawful had occurred. I was introduced to Les Brown. He wasn't a tall man. He looked up at me and said, "Son, they told me you were a sheriff, but I didn't believe it." He also said, "I don't usually play for just anyone. Doris Day recommended you to sing with us."

She was there. I was speechless. While standing there with him, I was having a flashback. I remember saying, when I was a young child, in the late forties and early fifties, that I was going to sing with Les Brown and his band. I was told back then to shut up because I talked like white folks.

I sang, in full uniform, with the orchestra. The fundraiser was a success. I sang songs that Doris Day made hits, back in the days. Mr. Brown came to me and said, "Son, you've got a set of chops. You can sing with me and my orchestra anytime. Let's take a picture together."

People from far and near heard me sing. I sang at a few hundred weddings, funerals, and fundraisers, and at professional baseball, football, and basketball games. I was sure that I was going to be somebody as a singer.

I had a woman ask me to sing at her father's funeral. I knew neither one of them. She said that both of them had heard me sing at a function, and they had been very impressed. Her father had asked her to have me sing at his funeral. There were countless requests like those. I even sang at a divorce ceremony.

My commander allowed me to sing at weddings and funerals, but I would have to use the thirty minutes allocated for lunch to perform these tasks.

Whenever I sang at the Carmel Mission, I would park my patrol car in the rear of the Mission and toss my gun belt in the trunk. I would go to the closet in the Mission, where I had a white robe. I would wear it over my sheriff's uniform when I sang. One of the fathers there told me that if I wore that robe for at least five more years, I would get a hood with two eye holes in it, like a Ku Klux Klansman.

Another time, I was singing at a wedding in a Protestant

church while on duty. For some reason, I had to stand on a stool to sing. While I was singing, the stool broke and I fell on the floor, but continued to sing.

Performing at a wedding at the Mission, I was again wearing my robe over my uniform. I had my handy-talkie attached to my gun belt with a Bluetooth in my ear. While singing Bach's *Ave Maria*, the dispatcher was telling me in my ear that a subject was threatening a party with a bayonet on a nearby beach.

Moments later, I finished singing and was like Clark Kent, changing into Superman. I ran to the closet, hung up my robe, went outside, put on my gun belt and arrived at the scene within two minutes from the call. There, I encountered a homeless man, who threatened to stab anyone who kept him from eating the food on a picnic table. This was at a company beach party. I managed to take the bayonet from him, place him under arrest, and then lodge him in the county jail.

I earned a reputation for singing operatic arias to prisoners when I transported them to the jail. Quite a few troublemakers hoped they would never have to ride in my patrol car because they did not like classical music I would sing while I was driving them to the jail.

Frequently I would sing the National Anthem at Little League games. Most of the time, a celebrity would attend. One year, a Carmel organization installed a new sound system at the local Little League field, but it didn't work at the opening of the game. I had to take my patrol car to the pitcher's mound and sing, using the car's sound system.

At some of these games, there were celebrity guests such as our own Leon Panetta. He was in the House of

Representatives in those days. Charlie Daniels, the country music legend, had advised me to retire from law enforcement before I got killed. He also said that I should be a professional singer, and that he particularly liked me because I was so patriotic. Each time I would get into a bad situation, I would think of him. I would open these games and he would often speak afterwards. Willie McCovey was also a guest at times.

"Doris Days' Best Friends" was a television show that this wonderful lady had on the air in 1985-86. Most of the shows were filmed in Carmel Valley where she lived. Many of her celebrity friends, such as Rock Hudson, were guests. One time I was a featured guest along with Angie Dickinson, and the president of Quail Lodge, Ed Haber. We filmed a wonderful show that was seen all over the nation.

Allen Funt, of the television show *Candid Camera*, lived on a ranch on the Big Sur coast and had the *Candid Camera* office in Pebble Beach. I was a guest on his show, too. He always attended my cabaret shows and wanted to hear "September Song." I sang that for him on his birthday.

John Denver leased a small castle-like home overlooking the ocean in Carmel Highlands. We became good friends. I would go with him to the different stores to purchase things that he needed for his home. Every other night he would play guitar at Clint Eastwood's Mission Ranch. He was just a regular person in this area. Whenever he went on tour, he would inform me of his entire tour schedule, and I was to contact his executive assistant in Colorado if there were problems at his residence. As everyone knows, he died young. He was only 53 when he went down in an experimental airplane into Monterey Bay near Lovers Point in Pacific Grove in 1997.

Clint Eastwood and I have been friends for almost forty years. He was my idol since he was as Rowdy Yates in the television series, *Rawhide*. Thanks to Clint, I am a member of the Screen Actors Guild. As I mentioned earlier, he gave me cameo parts in three of his movies. I also got to know his entire family, including his mother and step-dad, first wife, Maggie and their two children, Allison and Kyle, and his second wife, Dina.

I could go on and on about people I thought I would never meet but did, and there are some others I would have particularly liked to have met but never got the chance such as the late Howard Keel, Johnny Carson, and Burt Bacharach.

# <u>*More Sheriffing*</u>

A woman driving on the freeway hit a large buck but it was not killed. She was sitting on the side of the road, crying and holding its head. A deputy was dispatched to assist her. A very large deputy – he was called The Rock – drove up and slowly got out of his patrol car. The woman saw him and figured everything was going to be just fine. She thought that he would call someone from the SPCA to come get the buck and take care of it. The Rock was upset because it was so close to quitting time. He did not like getting calls close to quitting time.

He walked up to the woman and told her that she could leave if she wanted to. She wanted to stay. He asked her to step aside. Rock removed his .357 magnum from his holster and said, "The jig is up, Bambi," and shot it in the head. The buck died instantly. The Rock left. The buck wouldn't have lived anyway, and the quick death probably saved it some pain. The woman came unglued and started screaming. Just another story that shows that there are some strange folks on both sides of the law.

A cute teenage white girl from an upscale community was dating a Filipino against her parents' will. One night they told her not to see him ever again. She told the boy by telephone that she could not see him again. He was furious.

One morning a few days later, her father went to get the morning paper from the front yard. As he opened the front door, he saw a toilet seat with the cover closed on the doorstep. He picked up the toilet seat and noticed someone had pooped on the doorstep and covered it with the toilet seat.

I was patrolling in Carmel Valley one afternoon when I received a call about trespassers who were in the caller's tree. Minutes later, I arrived at her residence. She was standing in front of her house waiting for me.

She told me that eight white males had climbed up into a tall tree in her back yard and wouldn't come down. I thought this was really strange. We walked to the tree. I looked up and saw no one. She looked up and said, "All right you guys, I have the sheriff here. You'd better come down right now." I felt really sorry for this woman, as I have known her since she was a little girl. I knew that she had some mental issues, but I hadn't realized that they had gotten this much out of control.

I asked her to step aside, telling her that I would talk to them. I looked upward and shouted, "All right you guys, you've got a minute to get down here so we can talk." I waited for about three minutes. And then, as if they were standing at the bottom of the tree, I said, "Now you guys line up, shoulder to shoulder."

I pretended they were in a military formation. I stepped in front of them and began to lecture. I said, "I don't know why you guys came here to trespass on this property, but since I can't place you all in the back of my patrol car, meet me at the county jail. I think you should spend the night there. Now get going."

She thought that I was the greatest peace officer in the world for getting those guys out of the tree and off her property.

One cold afternoon, one of my colleagues received a call

in the Carmel Woods area. The caller said that he had not seen his neighbor, an elderly female, for the past two days. Each afternoon at four without fail, she would walk her little poodle. Every two to three days the deliveryman from a local market would deliver her groceries and leave them on her porch. For the past two days, neighborhood dogs had been eating the groceries. He was concerned because she lived alone and he thought maybe she was hurt.

I told my colleague, Jim Trega, that I would come to assist him. Another colleague said that he would come also but we told him, in a nice way, that we would handle it alone. This other officer could be very rude to elderly people. He ignored our suggestion and came anyway.

We found that both the front and back doors were locked. We found a key under the mat of the front door. We entered, walked in and noticed the resident, sitting in a chair with her legs crossed. She was dead. There were no tell-tale odors inside like gas or decomposition. She died while watching television probably two days earlier.

On an end table was a glass with her false teeth in it. Our no-mannered colleague looked into her opened eyes and said, "Didn't you know you were going to have company? Why didn't you have your choppers in your mouth?"

We told him to shut up but he kept talking. Her television was old and had a black and white screen. He said, "Why didn't you buy a color television set? You're cheap like one of our deputies in the office." He then went over to the fireplace mantel, removed the top from an urn containing her husband's ashes, and said, "Move over Henry, your wife is coming." At that point we told him that he had to leave.

I had a rookie with me on the Big Sur patrol one day. He was a country boy out of the Ozarks. He kept saying that he wanted to meet the legendary Walt Trotter. He had heard so much about him, but had never met him. I told him that we could probably stop by his house if we had the time. I went on to tell him stories about Walt.

As it happened, a few minutes later our dispatcher asked if we could stop by the Big Sur garage to pick up Walt. His Bronco wagon had broken down and had to stay at the garage for repairs. I told the rookie he was going to finally meet Walt Trotter. His eyes lit up.

We arrived at the garage where Walt was waiting for us. The rookie looked at Walt and said, "Damn, that's a big son-of-a-bitch." I told him not to say anything that would piss off Walt off because he had just finished a day's work and was tired and dirty. He also always wore his pants below his hairy waist line and wore size fifteen string up boots.

We had a rough time trying to get Walt into the back seat of our car because he was so big. We finally got him in and headed to his house.

Two miles uphill from the garage, the right rear tire blew on our sedan. I stopped near the maintenance yard at Cal-Trans. I opened the trunk, got the spare and handed it to Walt. He squeezed it, with his gigantic hands and said, "This son-of-a-bitch is low." He carried the spare with his middle finger in the hub and walked to the maintenance yard to fill it with air.

While trying to jack up the rear end of the car, I discovered that four teeth missing from the jack, making it impossible to raise the rear end. I asked my dispatcher to have "Mudflap" – that was our nickname for the tow truck driver – to bring a hydraulic jack to our location.

Just then, Walt returned with the spare tire. He said, "You don't have that tire off the rear yet?" I told him that I had a jack coming because this one was inoperable. He said,

"We don't have time to wait. I'm hungry." I told him we had no choice but to wait. I had already loosened the nuts on the wheel. Walt came up behind the car; lifted it up and said, "Now change the son-of-a-bitch."

Tourists were stopping and taking pictures and others were just watching. They could not believe his strength. The rookie himself just stared in disbelief.

We arrived at Walt's house. He invited us to eat with him. On his dinner table were fourteen pork chops, an extra-large wooden bowl of salad, a loaf of French bread, mashed potatoes, a large bowl of butter, a half-gallon of milk, and a whole pie. The rookie told Walt that he did not want to interfere with his family's dinner. Walt said, "They've eaten already, this is mine."

We kindly declined his offer and just had a cup of coffee before we continued our patrol. The rookie said that he could not believe Walt's appetite. He couldn't wait to tell the guys at the office at the end of the shift. They weren't surprised as they'd seen him eat.

I remember one day Walt and his brother, Frank, drove up a mountain trail in a small pickup truck. There was no room to turn around where it dead-ended, so one brother picked up the front while the other picked up the back of the pickup, they turned it around and drove back down the hill.

One Sunday morning, I received a call stating that a naked woman was in the parking lot at the Crossroads Center in front of the Bakers Square restaurant. She had been chasing people with a stick. I arrived at the scene and met this plus-size black woman putting on a pant suit. She had scattered her clothing over the north side of the restaurant parking lot. The restaurant was closed, with patrons inside peeking through the blinds. A witness told me she had been chasing people with a large stick in her hand and yelling obscenities. The manager had quickly locked the door to keep her out.

I gingerly approached her, aware that she was obviously mentally unstable. Whether it was drugs or a permanent condition, I had no way of knowing. She was standing against her vehicle, a Toyota station wagon. I said, "Hi, there young lady!"

She said, "I guess they sent you here to arrest me. Well, I will pull your arms out of your chest. I've hurt a number of policemen in my day. You were sent here because both of us are black." She was obviously angry as shown by the mean look on her face. I thought about what my strategy should be.

I told her that no one sent me to arrest her. I told her that I was just cruising along and saw her in the parking lot. I told her, "And I said to myself, 'there's the girl of my dreams!'" She smiled. I said to her, "I don't have a wife. When I saw you, I fell in love at first sight and decided to come over to talk to you." I told her that I was going to call my mother to let her know that I have finally found the girl of my dreams. I walked a few steps away and used my handy-talkie to speak with my dispatcher. She thought I was talking with my mother. I asked the dispatcher to send an ambulance to my location, but to park it out of sight from us on the west side of the Bank of America. No sirens or lights were necessary.

I also told dispatch that the EMT's should wait until I had her facing me. Then when I scratched my forehead, they would slowly come behind her with the gurney. My plan was to push her onto the gurney and they would strap her down. I also asked for them to send a couple of big EMTs as this woman weighed close to 250 pounds.

My backup was already there and was at the other end of the parking lot, out of her sight but watching my every move. Another deputy asked to come, but I asked him to come with no lights or siren.

The ambulance arrived and I saw that the attendants were very short and small. But they did exactly what I asked. The other deputy suddenly appeared and this caused the woman to jump into her car and lock the door. She said that I had lied to her and grabbed a large razor blade and threatened to cut me with it. I went to the car door and charmed her some more. She finally got out of the car, smiling again, but she still had the stick and the razor blade in her hands. I managed to lead her back toward where the gurney was. I scratched my forehead and the EMTs appeared quickly and quietly brought the gurney behind her.

Since she was out of earshot, I whispered to everyone that on the count of three, we're going to push her onto the gurney and strap her down. I counted then pushed her down on her back and they strapped her arms and legs to the gurney. She was screaming and yelling obscenities but she couldn't get loose. She was transported to Garden Pavilion at CHOMP and admitted. It turned out that she had been reported missing from a mental institution in the San Francisco area.

Ripplewood is a small resort located on Highway One in Big Sur proper where one can rent a cottage, dine at the restaurant, and purchase gasoline. On the property was a cage that housed a large Rhesus monkey named Herbie. He was a tourist attraction. On the cage was a large sign telling people not to get too close, especially if they were wearing glasses, because he would snatch them off a person's face. He had swings in his cage and seemed to enjoy swinging on them much of the time.

One day, someone gave Herbie some LSD. The cage he

was in had been thought to be escape proof, but Herbie went berserk, ripping the wire screen apart, climbing out of the cage, and running into the vacant lot. An employee, who was on the small side, grabbed Herbie, but could not hold him. The owner of the resort was very elderly and was bitten on the hand by Herbie and suffered a mild heart attack. Herbie stood in the middle of Highway One, beating his chest like an ape. Another employee finally managed to catch Herbie and took him to the veterinarian at SPCA.

An ambulance was called to transport the owner to the hospital. On its way to CHOMP, about ten miles north, in front of the Navy facility, the front wheel of the ambulance came off. They still got the owner to the hospital somehow. He was okay. Herbie came down from his trip and continued to entertain tourists.


One night, a deputy was checking an area where under-aged teens were known to go to drink beer. It was a pretty spot on a hill that overlooked the city of Monterey. The deputy checked the occupants of the parked cars, using his flashlight to check IDs. On the back seat of one car with two young men in it, he noticed a white plastic gallon bag. He had the two teens get out of the car and then he removed the bag.

The deputy told them that it looked like cocaine to him. He decided to take a little taste of it with his finger. The driver of the car tried to stop him, but was told by the deputy to be quiet. The deputy went ahead and tasted the powder, and then spat it out. He knew immediately that it wasn't cocaine, and asked the man what the heck it was. The driver said that he had tried to tell the deputy that he had just had his dog cremated and he was there to scatter the ashes over the cliff. He used to walk his dog up there every day.

A man called dispatch constantly to complain about trespassers walking on his vacant lot. The lot had very thick grass on it. Trespassers would walk over it to take a shortcut to town and leave their trash in the lot. Each time we did a check of the area, no one would be around. I suggested to the man that he buy some steel rakes and place them on the property so maybe the perps would clean up after themselves. I was kidding. But the man bought two dozen steel rakes and placed them in the grassy lot. He had no more problems, because when people would walk through the property, they would step on one of the rakes and the handle would fly up and hit them.

Another time when I was assigned to patrol Pebble Beach for a few weeks, a man invited me to come look at his vintage cars which he had stored in his four-car garage. While we were talking, I got a call on my radio to attend to a situation. I told the man that I would come back later that afternoon, after work.

Later that day, I was driving back in my own car, a small convertible with the top down. I stopped to say hello to a fellow deputy who was on the Pebble Beach patrol. He said that a resident had reported seeing a suspicious black male driving in the neighborhood. It was believed that he was casing the neighborhood, telling the dispatcher that several burglaries had occurred in the area during the past two months. The called suggested that a deputy check and identify this person. I told the deputy to tell the caller that I had already left the area.

The next morning I read the sheriff's log about the report the caller had made. While on patrol in Pebble Beach that day, I spoke with the caller and told him that I was the one he had reported acting suspiciously. I also said that no burglaries or thefts had occurred in that area in more than two years. His face turned beet red and he apologized. I told him he did the right thing by calling to report a suspicious person, adding that I would have done the same thing. I only wanted him to know that all black people weren't criminals.

A businessman in Big Sur asked my partner and me to keep an eye on his home construction site in Carmel Valley. He was in the process of building a new home by the golf course at the Quail Lodge Country Club. Whenever we were assigned to that beat, we'd check the site at least twice a shift, and we'd give him a regular progress report.

Three months later, the house was almost half-way done. Probably because we made so many area checks, no one wanted to come near the property. Six months later, the house was finished. Because the owner lived in Big Sur, he only came to the house every other week.

One night, we were patrolling in that area and I was the passenger. As we passed the house, we saw a light on in the kitchen. We knew that the owner was at his other residence in Big Sur. I told my partner that I had seen someone in the kitchen, and that it could be a burglar on the premises.

We parked the car just down the street from the house, walked to the front door, and quietly turned the doorknob. It was locked. We forced our way in and ran towards the kitchen. I grabbed the subject who was standing over the sink, turned him around and handcuffed him. I asked him if he knew the owner.

The man kept saying, "But, but, but...."

I told him, "I don't want to hear any 'ands' or 'buts.'" I asked him again if he knew the owner.

"But I am the owner," he said.

My partner and I looked at one another, and I said, "You're a liar." I continued to rough him up a little and was trying to get him to the patrol car.

Again he protested and said, "This is my house and I can prove it." So he showed us all the paperwork that proved he was the rightful owner. I then started to brush him off and apologized to him. We explained that we had watched this house being built for the past six months. The man brought to our attention that there was another house which was almost completed just around the curve at the end of the roadway.

He appreciated us having watched his house while it was being built. I gave him a business card with all of our office information. I told him he could file a complaint against us if he wanted. He said that he had no intentions of filing a complaint against us, and that he was gratified to see deputies in that area. Boy, were we relieved.

Afterwards, we went to the site of the other house and saw a vehicle owned by Don Tosh, the Big Sur owner, parked on the premises. We felt like fools. We had been watching the wrong house all of this time. Fortunately, there were never problems there.

A Carmel Valley resident was building a new home on the edge of a high cliff. He decided to look at the carpets that had been installed that day while he was at work. When he arrived, he noticed an old pickup truck in the driveway and the front door open. He thought the vehicle belonged to the carpet layer. He was concerned because he thought that the workman should not have been there that late; it was already six in the evening. As he walked through the door, he saw a man pulling up the carpet, and rolling it up, no doubt to remove it from the house. The man saw the owner come in. He ran outside on to the upper deck and jumped. Apparently, he did not know the area. He fell past the edge of the land and landed in a ravine.

When I arrived, the homeowner pointed out the area where he thought the suspect should be. With the help of some citizens, we found the suspect in a very bushy ravine with a broken leg. Without questioning him, he admitted to removing the carpet, saying he needed it for his own home. The ambulance arrived and he was transported to the hospital. Afterwards, he was lodged in the county jail, where they had no carpeting.

An old cowboy was having a problem with pranksters destroying his large roadside mailboxes. The boxes were mounted at the entrance to his ranch. He said that during the last month, three large mailboxes had been pulled down to the ground and run over by a vehicle. He asked the sheriff's office for area checks whenever possible.

It's a tough assignment that basically depended on luck, because the area was rural and we had a lot of territory.

So when we didn't have any luck, after losing another mailbox, the rancher decided to take matters into his own hands. He used his backhoe to make an elongated hole (12'x9'x5') in front of the new mailbox. He placed pieces of 5/8" plywood, and rolled grass over the plywood, to cover the hole. He had already contacted the postal service, advising them not to deliver, saying that he would have an employee pick up the mail at the post office in Salinas.

One weekend night, the rancher heard a loud noise all the way from the start of his driveway three-quarters of a mile to his house. He put on his clothes, grabbed his shotgun, and drove down to the road in his Jeep. As he got closer, he could see a cloud of dust in the moonlight.

When he arrived at the entrance, he saw a pick-up truck in the hole he had dug. No one was around, but the truck had been severely damaged. The pick-up was towed to a nearby garage. The owner was located by us running the license plate. He was a nearby teenage neighbor. He admitted to having destroyed the boxes, along with some friends, as a prank.

I was planning to have a barbecue at my house with some of my friends. Chuck Pius, (a.k.a. The Pope), lived in rural Carmel Valley close to the roadway. One day his little girl, Stephanie, ran into the house and announced that a pickup truck had struck and killed a large pig in front of their property. Chuck went out to check and sure enough, it was a large boar. He went into the house, telephoned my dispatcher, and asked her to tell me that my ribs were ready. She did, over the radio, and I got a lot of ribbing (sic) from my fellow deputies and the CHP.

One Sunday afternoon a neighbor reported a possible burglary at a residence in an unincorporated area of Carmel. I arrived at the address quickly and met the neighbor downhill from the residence in question. This residence was located on a hillside and had a long concrete driveway leading up to it.

The neighbor said that the owners were in Europe on vacation, and she had been collecting their mail and watching the house for them. She said that the suspect was still inside the house. She described him as being a white man, 25 to 35 years old, shoulder-length dirty brown hair, and wearing dirty clothes. She described him as "the hippy type."

I called for a backup and walked up to the front door. I noticed that the glass pane in the door had been broken. The suspect had apparently reached in, turned the doorknob, and entered that way.

I walked quietly inside. There was this God awful smell coming from the kitchen and the bathroom. I confronted the suspect in the kitchen. He did not get excited at all about seeing me. He appeared to be on some type of drug. I apprehended and handcuffed him, advised him of his rights, and placed him in the patrol car. Just then, the backup deputy, Richard Schmaltz, arrived. We checked the residence thoroughly. The suspect had taken a large stock pot and put everything from the refrigerator/freezer, the cabinets and the pantry into the pot, and it was boiling on the stove. That was that awful smell I encountered when I first entered.

Another part of the smell came from his feces which he had smeared on the walls of the bathroom and medicine chest. He had only been in there a short while but he'd done a lot of damage. When I interviewed him, he said that he was hungry and tired. He went to the house and knocked on the door. When he realized no one was there, he decided to break in. He was locked up in the county jail. A week later, the residents returned and determined he had done about $20,000 worth of damage to their home.

One day, two young men were talking, each telling the other how broke he was. One man told his friend that he knew where a rich old man – someone he did not like – lived in Carmel. He thought it would be a good idea to rob him. The friend also thought that it would be a good idea as he did not have a job. He was an unkempt hippy type, dirty and with long hair and a beard. His friend gave him the address in case he was interested.

About nine one morning, the suspect decided to go to the residence with intentions of robbing the old man. He rang the doorbell. The old man, wearing his bathrobe, answered the door. The suspect identified himself as the Fed Ex deliveryman. The old man looked and noticed how unkempt he was and not wearing a Fed Ex uniform. Also, the suspect had a gun in his waistband.

Then "FedEx" told the old man, "This is a stick-up." This as he tried to pull the pistol from his waistband. Somehow the gun was entangled in his clothing. The old man slammed the door in the perp's face, grabbed his wife, and ran outside through another door. The suspect opened the door and ran inside, but the layout of the house was really different from the average home. The suspect kept running into closets and pantries. The old man and his wife went downstairs and hid in their guesthouse. The suspect gave up, left the house and ran down the street. He did not have a vehicle.

The old man saw him leave and called the sheriff's office. Back-up deputies checked the neighborhood thoroughly and found him hiding underneath a large surf board that was leaning against the exterior of a house. The man was apprehended. His gun was taken and he was placed under arrest, read his rights, and was brought back to the scene where he was positively identified as being the suspect. Afterwards, he was transported and booked into the county jail.

All of the patrol cars could be started by one master key. If a deputy was locked out of his car, another one could come and unlock it. Shortly after midnight, two deputies were making a bar check at a favorite public hangout. Two other deputies decided to play a joke on the deputies making the bar check. One of the deputies unlocked their patrol car and laid down on the floor in the back so he couldn't be seen. The other deputy parked a short distance away and watched. A few moments later, the deputies came out and started their patrol car.

The deputies together in the car started off and were talking. Suddenly the deputy in the back on the floor said, "Got a match?" Both the deputies looked at each other, and were wondering who was talking. They laughed it off.

A few moments later, the deputy on the floor said, "Give me a match, please?" The driver of the car panicked. He thought it was a ghost speaking. He ran off the road and crashed the car. The damage wasn't major, and neither deputy was hurt. It was then that they saw the deputy in the back, who wasn't injured either. A report was written about the accident in the office. I think it said they had swerved to avoid a deer that was crossing the roadway.

"OTR" to the deputies patrolling midnights meant "Old Time Religion." When deputies decided they wanted to get together to, uh, exchange notes, one would call over the two-way radio and say, "OTR." That meant the deputies were to meet behind the Community Church in Carmel Valley.

This one particular night there were three patrol cars behind the church. They were parked side by side with the windows down so they all could talk to one another. This one night all of them fell asleep. One deputy's head was hanging out of the door, and he was sleeping so soundly that he slobbered on the side of the door.

After a while, someone started singing. One deputy woke up and saw a crowd of people standing around the patrol cars. He managed to get the other deputies awake. There were purses and tote bags on the hoods of the patrol cars. It was the Easter Sunday "Sunrise Service" and the people were singing the "Old Rugged Cross." The deputies were pretty embarrassed. They had to drive away slowly, in order to keep from hitting anyone in the crowd. Bless them all, no one reported that incident.

There was a man in the Carmel area who was good at making gadgets. One of his neighbors had told him that an alarm system was being installed in their residence, so he decided to make his own system. He thought about it for a while and came up with what he thought was a brilliant idea.

He found an old boxing glove at a garage sale. In his workspace at home he filled it with nuts and bolts. Somehow he managed to mount it nest to a door in the house. It was designed to strike an intruder, either on the side of the head or the body when they walked through the door. It was mounted on a very strong spring.

One night, he came home somewhat intoxicated. His wife was walking behind him and she tried to remind him about the glove he had set prior to leaving home. He ignored her. When he opened the door, the glove struck him on the side of his head, breaking his jaw. He had to have it wired up for quite a while. At least he learned that the gadget worked.

A married man who lived in an affluent community had been dating a wealthy widow for a number of years. He told her on many occasions that he was going to divorce his wife and marry her instead. Each time they dated, she would park about a block from his house so she could pick him up.

This one night they were having dinner at an upscale restaurant in downtown Monterey. They were having a discussion about his divorce. She told him that he had been saying he was going to divorce his wife for the past five years. So far, he had done nothing but make promises. She wanted him to get that divorce ASAP. An argument ensued. She tossed a drink into his face then her food. She pitched such a ruckus, that he decided she should take him home.

A short time later, she brought him near his home. There the argument continued. He got out of the car while she was talking, and he walked to his house. He went inside and greeted his wife as if nothing had happened. He had always told her that he was out with the boys.

The widow was still sitting in her car very upset. This particular car, a Chrysler Cordoba, had water in the bumpers. Rather than leave, she walked to his front door and used large rocks to break the stained glass windows that were on both sides of the door. The man was startled. His wife had no idea about the other woman and thought burglars were trying to get inside of their home. The widow ran and got into her car and drove a short distance from his home. She was still so upset, she drove into his driveway. He had a two-car garage that had individual doors. There was a support beam between the doors. She sped and struck the beam, backed up, and struck the beam again, causing the roof to cave in on top of his two Mercedes-Benz cars that were parked inside. She left for home, but water was on the concrete floor near the garage doors, indicating the front bumper of her car had been damaged.

The wife filed the report, but when I arrived at the house, the husband took me outside and told me the whole story. He didn't want his wife to find out. He said that I could probably find the widow at her home which was in a retirement community in Carmel Valley. He told me where she lived, but said he didn't want to file charges against her.

I checked the damage that was done to the front door. There were pieces of glass and two large rocks, scattered about the living room floor. The roof of the garage was sagging on top of the cars parked inside.

I went to her home in the retirement community. There, I saw that the front bumper that contained the water was damaged. She came to the door and invited me inside. She said that she was expecting me. She admitted having done the damage to his home, and she talked about the incident that occurred in the restaurant. She said that he had been lying about divorcing his wife for years. She was tired of him lying to her. She had her checkbook in her hand and said she would like to pay for all of the damages. I told her that she would have to discuss this matter with him.

I never did learn the outcome of this problem. He died a few years ago. He was a former peace officer.

In late winter 1995, the Monterey Peninsula had continuous heavy rainfall. In rural Carmel Valley, thirty-five miles out, water spilled over the dam, causing the river to rise three to four times its normal depth. The flood was rushing towards the ocean in Carmel. We had deputies in different areas evacuating residents.

Bridges were washed away along with earth and trees and everything else near the river. One property owner had a large shed that stored a few Ferrari engines and parts. The flood took the land under it, the shed, and all of its expensive contents down river. Several homes were severely damaged. All kinds of objects, such as propane tanks, refrigerators, motorcycles, sheds, lumber, and small cars were stacked against some of the bridges.

Planned communities along the river were flooded with the water rising three to four feet in some of the units. Some of the planned communities at the mouth of Carmel Valley were also affected, as were the Crossroads Center and some parts of the Carmel Rancho Center. One man hired a scuba diver to retrieve his golf clubs from a flooded underground parking garage.

The bridge at Highway One just south of Rio Road was completely washed away, preventing residents of Carmel Meadows to Big Sur and beyond from driving to their homes, except via narrow winding routes like Nacimiento Road, many miles to the south. A private helicopter flew residents from one side of the Carmel River to the other, for a fee. The Army Corp of Engineers worked 24/7 to replace the bridge by the summer tourist season.

It rained for days. The Red Cross and Salvation Army were assisting everyone who had suddenly become homeless. Also those who had been truly homeless, like those sleeping under bridges, had their places washed away.

I was told that the levee had washed away near the Mission Fields area. I was rushing to get the residents to evacuate in that area. Some left with only the clothes on their backs; others chose to stay. There were some who thought I was joking.

I saw the flood waters coming behind me. I watched in my rearview mirror, as the flood was right behind me, carrying different kinds of debris with it. I turned from Oliver Road, onto Rio Road, in an effort to reach Highway One, but I could not make it. The flood crossed the highway, came downhill and met me head on. There were all kinds of animals – deer, rabbits, rats, squirrels and others – swimming on top of the waters, trying to stay alive. My engine died immediately and flood waters were at window level and was seeping inside my patrol car. I was in the process of removing my uniform so I could swim. I had a handy-talkie and informed my dispatcher of my dilemma.

A few minutes later, a large Cal-Trans diesel trunk came through the flood in about four feet of water and backed towards my patrol car. The driver dove into the water and connected a large chain to the front of my car. Then he pulled me onto high ground on Highway One. My patrol car was full of water and could not be used for the next two months.

One sunny afternoon, a CHP Officer received a call to check on a stalled Mercedes-Benz convertible on Highway One in Carmel Highlands.

When the officer arrived, he saw a blonde in the driver's seat. He used his PA system in the front of his patrol car to give her instructions. He asked her to release her emergency brake and he would use his push-bumper to push her to the side of the roadway. She never turned around to look at the officer. All he could see was her long blonde hair.

He started to push the car, but it was difficult, because she had not released the emergency brake. He asked again for her to let up the brake and he pushed the car. She did not comply. Finally he gave it a good push. It rolled over the top of the embankment and came to rest about eight feet below. He rushed to assist the driver and met the blonde climbing up the embankment unharmed. The blonde was an Afghan dog! There were no people anywhere around.

Finally the owner of the car arrived at the scene with a mechanic from a nearby service station. She was very happy to see her dog not injured, but was quite upset about her car. She said that for some unknown reason the car stalled. She left the dog in the car to get help. It was the dog that was sitting in the driver's seat, and of course that was the reason why the emergency brake was not released. Fortunately, the car had only minor dents but it was mechanically sound. This matter was settled with the CHP.

I was patrolling Carmel Valley one Sunday morning. We were working shorthanded that day; only three of us. The Carmel deputy had to make an arrest in the Big Sur area and was in the process of transporting the prisoner to the county jail in Salinas. The Pebble Beach deputy received a call to go to the Catholic Church across from the monastery. A WMA had used his truck to crash into vehicles belonging to the nuns in their parking area. It was reported that he had driven the truck off the roadway and down into a ravine. I went to assist.

The driver was reported walking from the ravine, towards the highway. I got to the area quickly and saw a man walking south on Highway One just up the hill from the monastery. I was pretty sure that this man was my former neighbor. He closely fit the description given by the nuns. I had not seen him recently but had heard that he had left his family and was living in Carmel Valley with his girlfriend.

I did not want to believe it was my former neighbor, but I identified him as being the one who had caused the trouble. I pulled over and spoke to him in the same tone as I used to do almost on a daily basis. I noticed he was bleeding from his head and arms. At first he said that he was glad to see me. I saw that he seemed to be on some type of drug.

Suddenly he started to scream. He yelled, "You're not taking me anywhere, Pat." I asked him to calm down and for us to have a discussion. He started to run; I tackled him in the middle of the highway; he was trying to reach for my gun. I was in a dead radio area and had not been able to use my handy-talkie to call for help. None on the highway would help me. Most just drove around us. Tour buses stopped; the passengers got out taking pictures of us. We were right in the middle of the roadway on the yellow line.

His girlfriend came to the scene, I didn't know from where, and she jumped on top of the both of us. She was hitting me with her fist, yelling at me to leave him alone. He was still attempting to reach for my gun. Just in the nick of time Deputy Gregory Clark and an off-duty Secret Service agent from the San Jose area showed up. We managed to place him in the caged area of my car, but he kicked repeatedly, almost breaking the windows. EMT's arrived with an ambulance; he was placed on a gurney and strapped with leather restraints. He managed to break one of the straps. He was transported to CHOMP where medical personnel confirmed that he was under the influence of drugs.

I felt pretty bad because his kids were always at my house. He was a tile setter and was going to remodel my kitchen. Sadly, a few months later, he took his own life. Throughout this episode I was thinking of what Charlie Daniels had told me more than once. He said somebody I knew would try to kill me. I decided it was time to think seriously of retiring.

# *Moving On*

I retired from the sheriff's office in December of 1997 after 30 years of service. Bill Cassara set up a party to celebrate. First it was to be held at the Mission Ranch but so many people wanted to come that he decided to find a bigger place. They had it at Rancho Canada but even that was too small and hundreds of people who wanted to attend couldn't be accommodated. I have to say that it was a great event. Clint Eastwood was one of the speakers. They roasted me really good.

(Oh, and for the record, I never shot anyone in those 30 years, but there was a time or two that I got close.)

In 1998, I wasn't even 60 and I knew I had a lot of time left. I wasn't really interested in real estate, but a buddy of mine, Richard Whitworth, persuaded me to get my license and to work with him over at his office near the Crossroads. He was later killed in a motorcycle accident.

By then I had already gone to work for another realtor, Barbara Simmons, who had an office on Ocean Avenue, where we had a lot of tourist walk-ins. One day a guy came in and asked to talk to an agent. I told him I was an agent and asked him if he was interested in buying property. He said, "Well, I am, but this place is a little too liberal for me."

When Barbara retired in 2005, Judy Profeta from the Alain Pinel realty office called me. I told her that I didn't really know anything about real estate, that I was good with people, but that I wasn't good with numbers since my stroke. She told me she had a manager in her office who could handle the details, so I worked there for eight years.

One day I had floor duty and a man came in and asked to see an agent. I told him I was an agent and asked if I could help him. He said, "Nah, I don't think I like the lifestyles here." Then another time someone came in and when I told him I was an agent he said to me being black in this white neighborhood was going to be tough. He was right. Another guy came in and said, "I'd rather deal with my own kind." I heard a lot of remarks like that over the years, but I never reported them to my brokers. It wasn't that I was worried that they would fire me, but I didn't want them to think that I was whining.

It took me a while but I decided that I wasn't cut out for real estate. I realized that at 71 years old it was time to do what I really loved, which was singing. I am putting all my time and energy into being "The Singing Sheriff." The rest of me may be getting older, but not my voice and not my soul. I'm finding there are a lot of people who like to come see and hear me. I entertain them by singing it all – from opera to country and rock.

# *Afterword*

During the thirty years from 1967 to 1997 that I was with the Monterey County Sheriff's Department, I had quite a run. It would be easy to say that there were many experiences, good and bad, but that wouldn't begin to describe the scope and depth of what those years meant to me. In essence, I went from being an angry young black man afraid of white society – with reason – to being a grown man comfortable in his own skin.

I encountered many people who, to put it politely, had issues, but who, albeit indeliberately, were important to who I am today.

But I also met many fine people who helped me make that critical transition of becoming a man. Most important to me was Carol Zeise. We have been together since 1979.

While circumstances were often difficult, and far more so for others than myself, I recognize the enormous strides that our American society has made since my boyhood in Colored Town, and I'm proud to have been a small part of it.

Yes, we have a long way yet to go, but as the generations pass, I'm confident that hard work, pain, and suffering will produce results of which we can all be proud.

# *Thanks to...*

Thomas Oliver, Cathy Piefer, Patricia Ramsey, the California Rodeo Association, Chet and Marge Behen, Larry Tharpe, Mel Mason, Augustus Lewis, Ken Talmage, Ron Kurkendall, the Grainger Family, Helen Rucker, Col. Al Glover, Furman Sanchez, Bill and Ruthie Watts, Ron Weitzman and Morley Brown, Ken White, Chris and J. R. Shake, McKenzie Moss, William "Bill" Lemos, Brent Eastman, Richard and Susan Stephens, Billy De Berry, Steve Goldberg, Don Freeman, Mary Claypool, Monika Campbell, Jeanne Fromm, Brad and Mary Carl, Robert Profeta, Richard Atwell, Nick and Marilyn Hazovac, Dr. Robert Allen, Patrick DuVal, Sr., Bert Cutino and Ted Balestreri, Leon Panetta, Alf Clausen, Gerald Schroeder, Gene and Joan Vandervort, Monterey County Sheriffs Retirees, Robert Taylor, Carson Huntley, Julie Dalman, Alice Nunes, Rodney Fletcher, Rick Antle, Delberta Meyers, and Roger Chatterton.

# *Other Books from Seton Publishing*

*PARADISE POND* - A photographer and a college math professor meet serendipitously, and with thoughts and feelings explore a glorious future together.

*THE FRANCIE LEVILLARD MYSTERIES VOLUMES ONE THROUGH SIX* - short stories and an original play, featuring Francie LeVillard, the world's finest consulting detective.

*SELECTED WRITINGS* - Short stories and squibs; serious and humorous, from over the years.

*JENNIFER* – a social studies teacher is named a teach of the year. In Washington to receive her award, she speaks her mind to the president and puts her life on the line .

*TRINIDAD HEAD* – an English lit professor crosses the country for a new job to find out it's been pulled, but then discovers the real reason for his move.

*JUST IMAGINE* – a scintillating piece of fiction that tells the tale of a man returning from Heaven with a mission to tell Earthlings that they can see auras.

*THE AUTOBIOGRAPHY OF JOHN DOUGH, GIGOLO* – a novel about a former hedge fund manager who decides on a new path – to improve the lives of women. His clients include widows, divorcees and a gangster's moll.

*MAYHEM* – a contemporary novel set in Marin County, California, based on the mythic struggle between good and evil, with the author being called in to tip the tide of the titanic battle.

*SILVER LINING* – a novel about a shooting on the street that brings reporter David Skye and nurse Lucy Balfour together, for what becomes excitement and romance.

*THE OMEGA CRYSTAL* – a page-turner of a novel about how the petro industry is sitting on crucial developments in solar power, waiting until their inventories run dry.

*TRUTH BE TOLD* – a novelized version of a true story about an historic civil rights case of sexual harassment against a top-50 American law school.

*THE QUALITY INTERVIEW / GETTING IT RIGHT ON BOTH SIDES OF THE MIC* – a guide to the art of interviewing for interviewers and interviewees of every stripe.

*FROM TERROR TO TRIUMPH / THE HERMA SMITH CURTIS STORY* – a true story of surviving the Nazi *anchloss* of Austria to creating a successful new life on the Monterey Peninsula.

*DON'T MESS WITH THE PRESS / HOW TO WRITE, PRODUCE, AND REPORT QUALITY TELEVISION NEWS* - a guide to producing broadcast journalism.

*RIGHT CAR, RIGHT PRICE* - a simple guide that explains how to find, price, and buy the car or truck, new or used, best suited for your individual transportation needs.

Tony has also edited and published another ten books for clients. If you are interested in learning more, please visit

# SetonPublishing.com.